# Human Histology Practical Book With Text & Viva Questions

I0840488


**Dr. Sumit Tulshidas Patil**


Associate Professor

Department of Anatomy

Andaman & Nicobar Islands Institute of Medical Sciences,

Port Blair. 744104

Email- dr.sumitpatil1122@gmail.com

# Human Histology Practical Book

# With

# Text &  Viva Questions

**First Edition- 2019**

**Dr. Sumit T. Patil**

**Associate Professor**

**Department of Anatomy**

**Andaman & Nicobar Islands Institute of Medical Sciences,**

**Port Blair. 744104**

**Email-  dr.sumitpatil1122@gmail.com**

Copyright © 2019 Dr. Sumit T Patil

All rights reserved.

**ISBN:** 9781698968292

All rights of this book are reserved. No part should be reproduced or transmitted in any other form without written permission of the Author.

# CERTIFICATE

This is to certify that Mr. / Ms. ___________________________________

Reg.  No._______________  Year  _________  is  student  of  this  institute

___________________________________________________ has  attended  and

completed the practical  of Histology recorded in this journal in Anatomy.

**Signature of Teacher in charge**

   **Histology section**

**Professor and Head**

**Dept. of  Anatomy**

# INSTRUCTIONS

1) All the students must put on apron while working in histology laboratory.
2) Microscope should be handled carefully by the students. It should not be tilted too much.
3) Any damage to microscope or the slides must be reported immediately by the student to the technician of histology laboratory.
4) The student should bring this journal along with Haematoxylin & Eosin pencil, in every practical class.
5) The students must draw drawings during practical hours on the same day only. The signature of the teacher-in-charge must be obtained regularly at the end of practical hour.
6) Always try to label the diagrams on one side of the picture( usually on the right side)

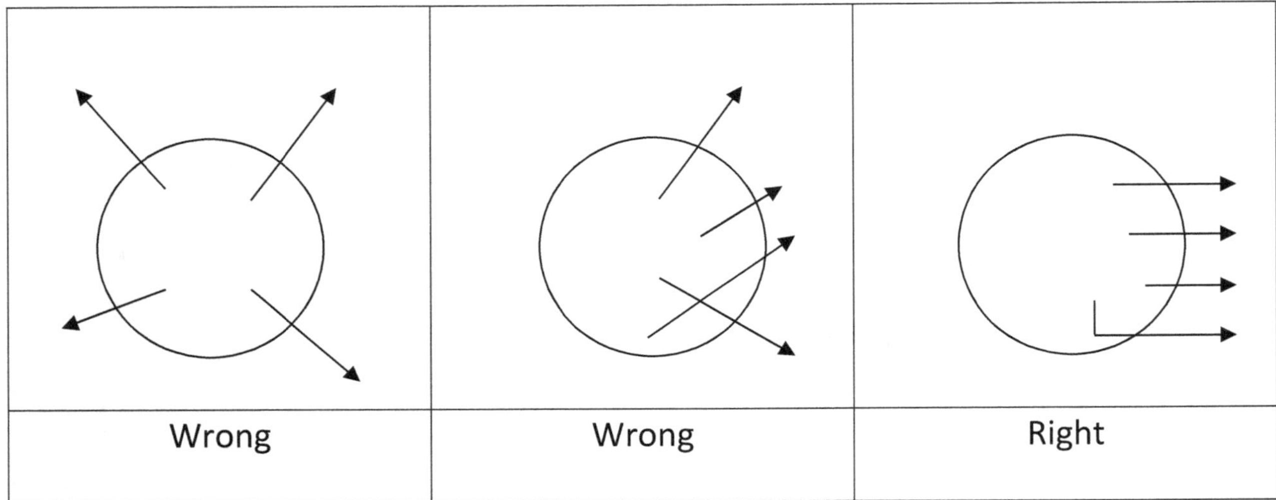



7) The Journal should be well- maintained and submitted with certificate of completion duly signed by the Professor of Anatomy, at the time of university exam.
8) In case of any difficulty or doubt the student should contact respective teacher-in-charge.

# INDEX

# CHAPTER No. 1
## HISTOLOGY TECHNIQUES AND MICROCOPE
### Histology Means Microscopic Anatomy

**Light Microscope:**

It is an instrument by which we study the minute details of tissue and organs. It has got the following different parts. Stand, Inclination Joint, stag for slide, tube, revolving Nose piece, Objectives, eyepiece, mirror (one side plane other side concave) and condenser. Here we use either natural light or special lamp is fitted with in the instrument. Light is transmitted through the section of the tissue.

**Certain Important Points:**

1) **Fixed tube** : Has a fixed length (160 m .m).

2) **Objectives** : There are three types of lenses.

a) Low power b) High power c) Oil immersion lens.

Each objective has magnifying power and focal length written on it. See it carefully.

Low power objective : X 10

16m.m. focal length.

High Power objective : X 43

4 m.m. Focal length.

Oil immersion lens : X 97

1.8 m.m. Focal length

3) Eye piece has got magnifying power written on it. It is marked as X5, X10, X20, X25. We use X10 Eye piece here. If, low power objective and an eye piece of 10 power is used the magnifying. Power of the microscope will be 10X10= 100 and so on.

The microscope has two functions.

1) Magnification. 2) Resolution.

Resolving power of microscope means clarity of image. If the resolving power of best optical microscope is 0.2 Micro meter then the microscope can show two particular particles distinctly even when they are separated by 0.2 Micro meter distance. The resolving power of the microscope is directly proportional to wave length of light and inversely proportional to numeric aperture (NA) of the objective.

**How to examine a slide**: - Note the following points carefully.

1) See the slide against light with naked eye. The observation tells the student whether tissue is solid (liver, kidney); tubular (G.I. tract etc) or ground bone or reticular tissue (silver impregnation).
2) Always use low power objective.
3) When you have seen complete structure under low power, then change the high power, to see detail. Cut off the light slightly by lowering down the condenser, e.g. striation of muscle, nuclear size, disposition etc.
4) Keeps the slide on the stage with the examination surface (i.e. cover slip) pointing towards objective, i.e. facing upwards.
5) If the tissue is not in view under high power, do not go on pressing the objective, as it may break the slide and damage the lens.
6) If the tissue slide is kept upside down (i.e. cover slip pointing down wards) it is impossible to focus the tissue under high power. Correct position of the slide then focus.
7) Condenser has a diaphragm fitted in it. The light can be controlled by diaphragm as well as by up & down position of the condenser.
8) Mirror: use plane mirror when condenser is up with Diaphragm open (more light). Use concave mirror with condenser lowered and cutting light with diaphragm (less light).

## OTHER MICROSCOPES:

Apart from the microscope used in the laboratory there are other microscopes.

### 1) Phase contrast Microscope:

It is used to see unstrained fresh living cytological preparation. It is based on the Refractive Index which measures the speed with which the material is traversed by light wave. Light wave traversing through air, water and glass, will emerge at different times in phase by phase. The phase contrast microscope consists of optical plates placed within the condenser and objective lenses which convert the phase differences in to amplitude differences. Here light ray passing through different parts of cell from different phases and then transformed into light intensities and image becomes visible.

**2) The polarising Microscope:**

It is used to distinguish between monorefringent and birefringent substances. Monorefringent substances are amorphous or non crystalline and do not divide the light ray. (Non-Polarisation) while birefringent substances are crystalline and divide the light ray (polarize) into two; one ordinary and other extra ordinary ray. In the polarising microscope the extra-ordinary ray are utilized image. Hence monorefringent are not visible but birefringent are visible in this microscope. In the biological specimen, crystalline substances of bone tissue; linear symmetry of collagen, muscle fibre; nerve fibre, cilia etc. are nicely seen with polarizing microscope.

**3) Electron Microscope:**

It has got very high resolution power, by which structures very close to each other (say 1nm distance apart) can be seen nicely with 200 times greater magnification than light microscope.

Here instead of light, electrons are used and in place of glass lenses electromagnetic fields are used. Electrons passing through a very thin object 0.2 to 0.1 micrometre thick are deflected by electromagnetic fields (like glass lenses in light microscope) and are focussed on a photographic plate for a photograph to be taken. Electron microscope has enabled us to study cellular details. It has two type of working.

a) Transmission Electron microscopy, showing the details of cells.

b) Scanning electron microscopy, showing the surface of cells.

**Units of measurements:**

**Units of measurements used in light microscopy**

1) Micron(Micrometre) =     $1\mu$ or $1\ \mu m = 10^{-6}$ m  or  0.001mm

**Electron Microscopy.**

2)  Angstrom =  $1A^{\circ} = 10^{-10}$m   or 0.1 nm (Nanometer)

3) Nanometer =  1nm $= 10^{-9}$  or 0.001 micron

# STUDY OF TISSUE

Any tissue can be studied by following various methods:-

**1) Examination of fresh cells** - i.e. a drop of blood, lymph, C.S.F. Stools, Urine, pus in fresh state.

**2) Dissociation or teasing method** - Tissue or organ cells are separated from each other by fine dissecting needles in a fluid medium then stained and observed.

**3) Smear technique** - Fresh specimen is spread on the slide, fixed, then stained and seen under the Microscope.  e.g. blood sugar.

**4) Sectional method** - This is most common method of studying the tissue. The tissue is passed through various processes; a paraffin wax block is made and then cutting to very fine section, mounted, stained and seen under the microscope.

**5) Vital staining**- (a) Supra vital staining : the tissue is put into  staining fluid and stained enblock,  e.g. staining of mitochondria.

(b) Intravital staining: Here the harmless dye is injected into the living organism and then, after dissection the tissue is seen under the microscope, e.g. kuffers cells in liver.

*************************

## SECTIONAL METHOD

This method includes following steps:

Fixation, Dehydration, Clearing, Paraffin embedding, Section cutting, mounting the section on slides and staining.

1) **FIXATION**: The tissue should be fresh and normal. Autolytic degenerative changes occur after 6hrs. of death. Mammalian tissue is good for study. Human tissues are obtained from operation theatre or post-mortem room.

**What is fixation?** It is the presentation of tissue in as natural and as life-like condition, as possible. This is done before any degenerative changes take place in the tissue.

**What are Fixatives?** These are the various chemicals used either single or in combination in form of solutions.

**Common fixatives** used are formalin, Mercuric chloride, Osmium tetra oxide, Chromic acid, Potassium Dichromate, Acetic acid, Picric Absolute alcohol.

**Common Fixative solution used:-**

a. Formalin Solution.
b. Formal saline.
c. Bouins fluid.
d. Zenkar's solution.
e. Heldenha Susa.

TYPES OF FIXATION-

1) **Micro Anatomical:** Used for preserving the relations of the tissues. This is a routine method, for histological study.

2) **Cytological:** For preserving the cellular elements. This is used in Histochemistry.

## Following are the steps of sectional method

1) **Fixation-** This depends on the thickness of tissue taken, thinner the tissue, less the time. The time varies from 1 to 14 hours.
2) **Dehydration**: Tissue is fixed & then dehydrated to remove water. This is done by keeping the tissue in ascending grades of alcohol; like from 70; 90; and absolute.
3) **Clearing**: this means removal of alcohol from the tissue by keeping in clearing agents like benzene; cedar wood oil, xylol. The alcohol is replaced by clearing agent and it is miscible with paraffin wax of which blocks are prepared.
4) **Paraffin embedding**: The tissue once appears transparent, and then it is cooked in paraffin. Cooking time depends on size of tissue. Cooking removes clearing agent and is replaced by paraffin.
5) **Making Paraffin blocks**: The tissue is kept in L-mould cube box; melted paraffin poured to fill the box and then allowed to cool. Paraffin is now hard and can be cut by knife.
6) **Section cutting**: The block is put on a microtome to cut the fine section of the tissue with the help of a knife. 5 to 10mm thick sections are cut in a ribbon.

**7) Mounting**: Single section is put on albumenised slide with some water. The slide is warmed to flatten the section. Water is removed, so that section attaches to the slide. This slide is allowed to dry. Now it is ready for staining.

## STAINING

The cellular details of the tissue cannot be clearly seen as they are. Hence, in order to visualise them in details, staining is required. Different constituents of cell have special affinity for certain dyes. The nucleus of the cell is stained by basic dyes like Haematoxylin (Blue-black) as the nucleus contain DNA (Acid) and the Cytoplasm is stained by acidic stains like Eosin (pink) as the proteins of the cytoplasm are basic in nature.

**IMPREGNATION:** is a different process, and is done by inorganic salts, which are deposited on the particular part of cell, rendering it opaque and black, silver Nitrate is most commonly used. E.g. reticular fibres, impregnated with silver-nitrate, appear jet black.

## STAINS

1) **Micro anatomical:-**This stains the tissue elements in general for histological study.
2) **Cytological:** - used for the demonstration of certain particular of cell. Best carmine is used for demonstrating the Glycogen of the cell.

**Specific stains**: - Certain elements of tissue are stained only by particular stains. These specific stains are orcein for elastic tissue; scharlech R-Sudan lll, and osmic-Acid for fatty tissue and light Green for Collagen fibres.

## COMMON STAINS USED

**Haematoxylin** – (Nuclear stain)
Make a sat. sol. Or 50/n of ammonium alum, boil, cool, keep for 24 hrs, and filter. Take calcium chloride 10gms. Add 100 c.c distilled water stand for 5 hrs with occasional shaking and filter. Take 55gms of haematoxylin in 5 c.c absolute alcohol and 20 c.c of calcium chloride solution. Add 70 c.c of saturated Ammonium alum solution with shaking vigorously, and 5 c.c glacial acetic acid. Haematoxylin is ready for use.

**Other Dyes-**

       Eosin - 1% aqueous sol. (Protoplasmic stain)
       Methylene blue 1% sol. (nuclear stain)
       Neutral red 0.5 % sol (nuclear stain)
       Van Giesons stain (different stain for connective tissue)
       Acid fuchsin - Elastic Fibres.
       Silver nitrate-Reticular tissue.

# MOST COMMON COMBINATION OF TWO STAINS USED ONE AFTER ANOTHER

1)    Haematoxylin and Eosin
2)    Haematoxylin and Fuchsin
3)    Haematoxylin and Van Giesons
4)    Methylene Blue and eosin
5)    Acid Fuchsin and Methylene Blue
6)    Neutral Red and Methylene Blue

**Note:** -the first stain is used for 5-10 minutes the second for ½ to 2 minutes.

**DOUBLE STAINING PARAFFIN SECTION**

- Warm the slide enough for paraffin to melt.
- Put on Xylene at once. Repeat twice, to remove paraffin.
- Then put absolute alcohol followed by.
- 90 % alcohol  followed by
- 70% alcohol fallowed by
- Distilled water.
- Move excess water.
- Stain with Haematoxylin for 5 to 10 minutes.(Nuclear stain nuclei Blue or Black)
- Wash in tap water till section become light blue.
- Remove excess water.
- Stain with Eosin for ½ to 1 minute. (Cytoplasmic stain cytoplasm Pink)
- Dehydrate with
- 70% Alcohol.
- 90 % Alcohol
- Clear in Xylene
- Mount in D.P.X.

## QUESTION

1) How will you know the magnifying power of microscope?
2) What do you mean by resolution power of microscope?
3) Stained tissue slide is kept upside down on the microscope stage?
   a) Will you be able to visualize under low power?
   b) Will you be able to visualize it under high power? If not? Why not?
2) Why paraffin embedding is necessary for the tissue?
3) What is microtome? What is its necessity?
4) What is Micron?
5) What is a nuclear stain? Give an example.
6) What is cytoplasmic stain? Give example.

# 1. Microscope

# CHAPTER 2. CELL

The human body like other animals and plants is made up of functional & structural units called cells. Cells vary greatly in their structure and a study of cell's structure is called "cytology"

**Tissues:** Tissue of the body means aggregation of cells of common or same type. There are four basic types of tissues in the body.

1) **Epithelium** – which covers or line the external or internal surface of the body? Epithelium consists of single or multiple layers of cells. Main functions of epithelium are protection, absorption, secretion etc.
2) **Connective tissue-** which connects or binds different cells or tissues. Function is to support, bind and protect various tissues.
3) **Muscular tissue-** consists of muscle cells. The property of tissue is contraction.
4) **Nervous tissue-** This tissue carries important messages by conduction from and to the brain and spinal cord.

**Organs-** organs are made up of combinations of different types of tissues. As for example in the wall of stomach all four kinds of basic tissue are observed.

**Structure of cell:**
1) **Morphology of cells:**
   a) **Shape-** Cell may be flat, discoid (red blood cell) columnar; pyramidal; spindle; stellate. The shape may be changeable as with amoeba (single cell animal), leucocytes (white blood cell) or macrophages. Some cells are very long e.g. muscles cells; nerve cell.
   b) **Polarity-** the constituent part of cell has a definite special arrangement in cell with respect to each other and the cell as a whole. E.g. location of nucleus is correlated with size and shape of cell and also with deposition or other elements like mitochondria; R.E.R. & SER; Golgi apparatus etc. This arrangement illustrates the cellular structure polarity.
   c) **Size-** cells are microscopic. Some are visible to naked eye. E.g. many eggs (ova). Some cells are giant cells; e.g. megakaryocyte of bone marrow. Some are multinucleated cells. This is also called syncytium. There is no

correlation between the size of animal and size of cell. The amphibian cells are larger than mammalian cells.

d) **Numbers-** the size of the animal depends on the number of cells. Total number of cells in larger animals being more than in a small animal.

e) **Specialization or differentiation-** the cells modify their structure according to specific functions. This process is called differentiation. With high differentiation there is a loss of basic property like multiplication. Hence; nerve cells; highly differentiated; once damaged cannot be replaced by other nerve cell (by multiplication of existing cells) but by fibrosis and there is loss of function.

2) **Cytoplasm-** it is a special kind of protoplasm. It includes all protoplasm of a cell except that of the nucleus.

a) **Plasma membrane-** it is a cytoplasmic boundary. With light microscope appears as a thin line. With electron microscope, a trilaminar structure is seen. The trilaminar structure is called unit membrane. The trilaminar structure seen in electron microscope is because of arrangement of lipid molecules. The globular heads which are hydrophilic form the dark lines while the thin part of the molecules forms the faint hydrophobic central region. In addition to lipids there are proteins molecules present here and there in the cell membrane without any specific arrangement. Some of them come on the surface. Some occupy the whole thickness of the membrane.

1) **Functions of plasma membrane-**

The plasma membrane controls the entry into the cells of fluid and micro or macromolecules (by phagocytosis). Thus, it is a semi permeable membrane determining the exchanges accruing by osmosis or phagocytosis. The plasma membrane is tough & elastic. Animal cell has a glycoprotein; covering the surface of the plasma membrane called CELL COAT. It holds the cell together. The secretion of the cell is related out by a process exocytosis. (Reverse of Pinocytosis).

**Pinocytosis-** drinking process of a cell. (Fluid intake)

**Phagocytosis-** eating process of cell (solid intake).

2) **Some other functions of cell membrane –**

a) Form a sensory surface e.g. in muscle & Nerve cell. Depolarization of the membrane (selective passage of sodium & potassium ions across the membrane) results in contraction of muscle and conduction of nerve impulse.

b) The surfaces of the cell membrane bear enzymes which affect the activity of the cell.

c) May show high degree of specialization as with rods and cones cells of retina (Proteins sensitivity to light)

3) **Cell organelles-** (as seen with E.M.)

Organelles are suspended in the cytosol; the protein suspension of cytoplasm.

1) **Endoplasmic reticulum-** forms the membranous sacs or tubules with various biochemical processes and also carbohydrate metabolism.

2) **Ribosome-** small bodies of protein & RNA, present in the cytoplasm either single (Monosomes) or in groups (Polysomes) are associated with RER. Ribosome helps in protein synthesis.

3) **Mitochondria-** are small granules or rods. They can duplicate themselves during cell division. Each mitochondrion has outer membrane bag, in which there is inner bag folded upon it forming shelves called cristae. The inner bag contains matrix containing enzymes. The enzymes provide energy for various cellular functions. Hence mitochondria are called power houses.

4) **Golgi complex-** it is near nucleus; consists of smooth membrane sacs stacked one over another, Golgi complex forms secretary product mainly carbohydrates (Glycogen). Golgi complex forms the packing unit for secretion of RER. The secretion granules combine with glycogen here and packed before release.

5) **Membrane bound vesicles-** the cytoplasm of a cell contains the following vesicles.

**Phagosomes-** Consist of solid foreign material engulfed by the cell.

**Pinocytotic vesicle-** the fluid taken in by the cell by a process called Pinocytosis.

**Exocytotic vesicle-** particles produced by the cell are released out of the cell by a process called exocytosis.

**Lysosomes-** contain enzymes which can digest the Phagosomes (e.g. bacteria). The Lysosomes fuses with Phagosomes and destroy the harmful material.

6) **Microtubules and microfilaments-** the elongated elements in many cells are called microtubules which are tubular and hollow while microfilaments are solid filaments. Both consist of protein tubulin and actin respectively. They form the cytoskeleton of cell, as in nerve cell and form the spindle during mitosis.

7) **Centriole-** Light microscope shows them as two small dots; E.M. shows as two small rods at the right angles to each other. Each rod consists of nine triplets of microtubules. Centriole form mitotic spindle, cilia, flagella, tail of spermatozoa etc.

**Projection from cell surfaces:**

1) **Cilia-** Light microscope shows them as hair like projections. Details with E.M. show each cilium has a central core of microtubules, nine doublets with a central doublet. This case is covered by cell membrane. The cilia are attached to cell at the basal body which has a structure similar to Centriole. Cilia produce wave like movement and help in moving the object in a fixed direction e.g. cilia of respiratory tract move the mucous to exterior; uterine tube cilia move the ova towards uterine cavity.

2) **Flagella-** It is a long cilium e.g. tail of spermatozoa. The movement is different than ciliary movement which can be compared to the movement made by a snake.

3) **Microvilli-** They are finger like projections from cell surface consisting of a central core of cytoplasm covered by cell membrane. There are number of microfilaments to hold the Microvilli. Number of enzymes is associated with Microvilli. Best example is the brush border seen with epithelium of small intestine in light microscope; with EM it is clear that it is formed by Microvilli regularly arranged.

4) **The nucleus-** In H & E stained slide the cytoplasm is stained pink while nucleus is stained dark blue. Usually centrally located in the cell; Nucleus has a nuclear membrane which is a double layered structure. It separates nucleus from cytoplasm; but because of the presence of pores in the membrane; there is to & fro communication between nucleus and cytoplasm. When the nucleus contains DNA (deoxyribonucleic acid) and proteins called chromatin, nucleolus & nuclear matrix. When the nucleus is large & the chromatin fibres loosely arranged, the nucleus is called open face or vesicular nucleus. The loose chromatin is called

Euchromatin, which indicates the actively functioning cell. On the other hand when the chromatin is condensed and forms compact mass it is called Heterochromatin. It is a closed face nucleus. The DNA of the nucleus forms the chromosomes (condensed rod like structures) during cell division. The DNA controls the activities in the cytoplasm by sending messengers in the form of messages RNA to the cytoplasm.

**Nucleoli**- are very small darkly stained bodies present in the nucleus. They may be one or more. Nucleoli are sites for the RNA (Ribosomal RNA) synthesis; which is produced here and then transported to cytoplasm through nuclear pores.

**Nucleoplasm**- The various constituents of the nucleus are held together by a base called Nucleoplasm.

**Chromosomes**- there are 23 pairs of chromosomes in human being. 22 pairs are called autosomes. One pair is called sex chromosomes. In females this pair is XX while in male it is XY. In females one of the X is active, other not functioning condensed to a compact mass in the nucleus called sex chromatin by identification of which the nuclear Sex can be identified. It is called as "Barr body". Sex chromatin may be seen as Plano-convex mass just deep to nuclear membrane in cells or it may form a drumstick as with polymorph nuclear cells. Chromosomes carry genes which are responsible for transmission of characters.

## QUESTIONS

1) What are the different shapes of the cell?
2) What is the relation between size of the animal and the number of cells?
3) What are organelles? Name them?
4) What do you know about cilia; flagella and Microvilli?
5) What is "Barr body"?
6) What are the properties of a cell membrane?
7) What are the colours taken by the nucleus and cytoplasm in H & E staining and why?

# 2. The Cell (E.M.)

# CHAPTER 3.  EPITHELIUM

**Definition-** It is a continues sheet of cells made up of single or multiple layers of cells which line an external or internal surface, with very little intercellular space. Cells are supported by a basement membrane consisting of very fine reticular fibers.

Epithelium arises from all the three embryonic layers i.e. Ectoderm (Epidermis); Mesoderm (Peritoneum) and Endoderm (Epithelium of GT tract).

## CLASIFICATION

1.  GLANDULAR EPITHELIUM
2.  SURFACE EPITHELIUM

**1) Simple Epithelium**
Single layer of cells

**2) Pseudo stratified Epithelium**
False impression of many layers of cells

**3) Stratified Epithelium**
More than one layers of cells

Simple squamous.

Simple cuboidal.

Simple columnar.

As the cells seen in vertical section of simple epithelium.

**Simple squamous-** is also called pavement epithelium. Cells are flat, have length, breadth, but little thickness. Imagine fried eggs lay in tray side to side.

**Site -** Bowman's capsule, Lining of Peritoneum, Pleura, Pericardium, Endothelium of heart & blood vessels, Alveoli of Lungs etc.

## Simple columnar

**Columnar cell-** Height is more, breadth less, tapering at base, broad at free end, nucleus in the middle of the cell. Gaps between the cell bases are filled by basal or packing cells.

**Goblet cell-** Some columnar cells take up the function of secreting mucus. Cells filled with mucinogen granules. When fully packed become bloated, swollen and then, bursts.

It gives out secretion and return to normal columnar cell. Goblet cells are stained faint blue because of mucous in H. & E. staining.

**Ciliated Columnar Cell-** looks like simple columnar cell but has cilia (Hair like processes) at the surface. Cilia have a typical structure with microtubules in the core which are present in Microvilli. Cilia beat to and fro rapidly in a consistent direction and remove the foreign particles.

**Site –** Alveoli of most of the glands of the body germinal epithelium of ovary.

## SIMPLE CUBOIDAL EPITHELIUM

**Cuboidal cell-** Is like a closed box with equal sides and six surfaces.

**Site -** Alveoli of most of the glands of the body, germinal epithelium of ovary.

# STRTIFIED (COMPOUND) EPITHELIUM

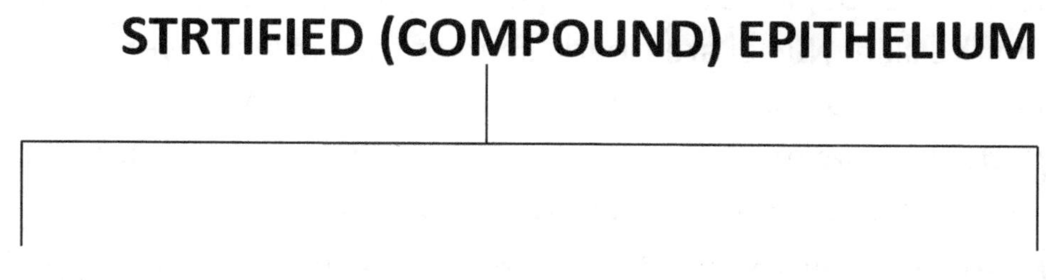

**1. PSEUDOSRATIFIED**

**2. STRATIFIED**

1. **Pseudo stratified epithelium:**
   a) Have three types of cells, columnar, pyramidal; basal.
   b) All cells touch basement membrane (IMP).
   c) Nuclei of these cells lie at different levels.
   d) Various positions of the different cell nuclei give impression of many layers of cells. Hence the name pseudo stratified.
   e) Pseudo stratified ciliated columnar epithelium is present in human trachea and bronchi.
2. **Stratified Epithelium:** Multiple layers of cells
   1) Transitional Epithelium
   2) Stratified Columnar Epithelium.
   3) Stratified Squamous Epithelium.
   4) Stratified Cuboidal Epithelium

1) **Transitional** - 3 to 4 layers of cells, pear shaped Umbrella cells on the surface. It is present in organs subjected to Stretch and pressure and required a non absorbing surface. It can Stretch and produce a non absorbable surface.
   **Site** -Urinary bladder, ureter, pelvis of Kidney,

2) **Stratified columnar** - (Male and female urethra) 2 to 3 layers of cells, Surface layer is always columnar cell layer.

3) **Stratified Squamous:**
   a) **Moist-** (12 or more layers) found in oesophagus, cornea; oral cavity and anal canal etc. Deepest layer is low columnar; produces cells which go to the surface. Superficial layers are of squamous cells. It is not keratinised as in the skin. Nuclei are clearly seen of the surface layer cells.
   b) **Dry:** (12 or more layers) Found in skin as Epidermis.
      1) Deepest layer- Stratum Basale consisting of low columnar / cuboidal germinal cells on the basement membrane.
      2) Stratum spinosum- several layers of polygonal cells with tonofibrils.
      3) Stratum granulosum- 3-5 layers of flattened cells with keratohyalin granules take basophilic stain.
      4) Stratum Lucidium- seen in thick skin only. Cells are flattened, translucent, eosinophilic without any cell organelles.
      5) Stratum corneum- the surface, keratinised layer of the cells which are dead, no nuclei seen.

**Functions of Epithelium:**

- **Protective** - Skin; membrane of mouth, oesophagus, anus etc.
- **Secretary** - Intestinal glands, salivary glands, Goblet cell.
- **Excretion** - Urine, sweat etc.
- **Absorption** -Intestinal epithelium, lung alveoli, kidney tubules.
- **Lubrication** - Peritoneum, pleura, pericardium.
- **Sensory** - Taste, hearing, smell, touch(skin)
- **Reproductive** - Germinal epithelium.

**Blood supply -** Epithelium is not supplied by blood. Nutrition of cells is carried through the tissue fluid by diffusion.

**Nerve supply-** Epithelium is profusely supplied by nerve fibres through free nerve ending.

# Epithelium Replacement & Repair -

Epitheliums are subject to wear and tear. Epidermal & Intestinal cells are shed regularly. The cells are replaced by some other cells at the basal layer having capacity to multiply in the stratified epithelium. Cells are produced in the basal layer and then go towards the surface gradually. In simple epithelium, mitotic cells lie side by side.

**Free surface of epithelial cells show with E.M**

I. **Cilia-** motile, 5- 10 Micrometer length; propel foreign particles in one direction towards exit. Present in respiratory tract and fallopian tube. In the core of cilia there are 20 microtubules arranged in 10 pairs. One pair is present in the centre and nine at periphery.

II. **Microvilli-** very minute; 0.5 to 1 Micrometer in height, finger like process coming from cell surface to increased the absorptive surface area e.g. small intestine(striated border of the light microscope) Microvilli have very fine filamentous support cytoskeleton.

III. **Stereo cilia-** Are long microvillus and NOT CILIA proper. They have the structure of Microvilli.They are present in male genital tract (Epididymis). Function mainly adsorptive.

**Cell junction-** epithelial cells are held together by junctional complexes and not by intercellular cement.

I. **Tight junction** – Present nearer the luminal surface. Forms complete circumferential belt around each cell. Here the outer lamina of plasma membranes of opposing cells fuse and thus seal the inner cellular space from the lumen.

II. **Adherent Junction-** Not a tight junction. Fusion of plasma membrane only.

III.  **Desmosomes-** Occur singly at many places. Between the opposing cell surface many fine transverse filaments are seen.

IV.  **Gap Junction-** Broad area of closely opposed plasma membranes. No fusion of cell wall. The narrow gap permits passage of ions and help in intercellular information exchange.

**Basement Membrane-** seen as homogeneous; layer in light microscope. Two basic layers.

a)  Basal lamina in contact with cell.

b)  Reticular lamina in contact with deeper connective tissue.
Basement membrane with H & E appears as single line (pinkish), with special stain like PAS it is stained prominently.

## GLANDS

Glands are specialised epithelial cells to perform secretary function. These cells may be singly present or in groups. Hence glands may be (1) Unicellular (2) Multicellular.

1) **Unicellular Glands:**
Goblet cells are unicellular glands. They are present in respiratory and GI tract. They secrete mucous which covers the epithelium and protects. They are placed in between epithelial cells. Goblet cell is narrow where it is resting on basement membrane and widens above where mucous collects. The nucleus is present at base. The typical shape is the reason, for its name "Goblet".

2) **Multicellular glands:**
They develop as diverticula from surface epithelium. The distal part of the diverticulum develops into the secretary glandular portion while the proximal portion  opening on the epithelial surface form the duct. Multicellular glands may be.

a) **Exocrine-** here the connecting duct functional and carry the secretions to the surface.

b) **Endocrine-** here the connection between secretary portion and the surface epithelium (i.e. Duct) disappears. The secretary portion forms then the endocrine (ductless) gland and pours the secretion directly in the blood circulation.

## Classification of Exocrine Glands

**A) Based on Shape & Branching Pattern-**
**1) Simple Glands-**
- Simple Tubular  - eg. Crypts of Lieberkuhns / intestinal glands
- Simple coiled Tubular- eg. Sweat Gland
- Simple Branched Tubular-  eg. Fundic Glands of Stomach
- Simple Alveolar- eg. Mucous Gland of Urethra
- Simple Branched Alveolar – eg. Meibomian Gland

**2) Compound Gland –**
- Compound Tubular – eg. Brunner's gland of duodenum
- Compound Alveolar – eg. Mammary Gland
- Compound Tubulo-alveolar – eg. Submandibular gland

**B) Based on mode of release of secretions**
- Merocrine – Secretions are released by the process of exocytosis in the form of secretory granules. Eg. Pancreas, Parotid gland
- Apocrine -  Apical portion of cell consisting of secretions is pinched off. Eg. Lipid component of milk in mammary gland by apocrine process & protein component is secreted by merocrine process.
- Holocrine – whole cell is secreted as secretion. Eg Sebaceous gland

**C) Based on Nature of secretions**
- Mucous Gland- eg. Sublingual gland
- Serous Gland – eg Parotid gland
- Mixed gland- eg Submandibular gland

## SIMPLE SQUAMOUS EPITHELIUM (LUNG)

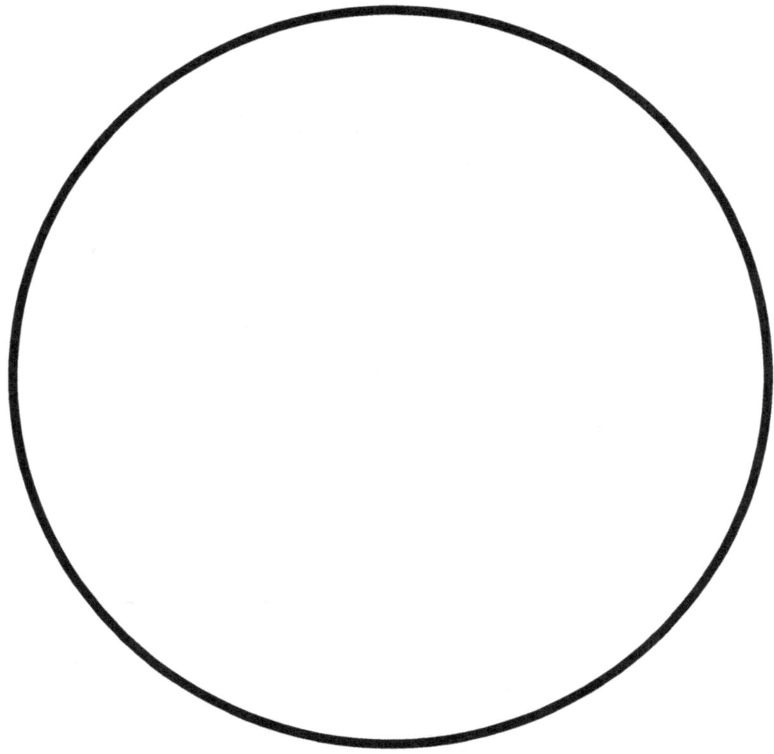

## SIMPLE CUBOIDAL EPITHELIUM (Thyroid)

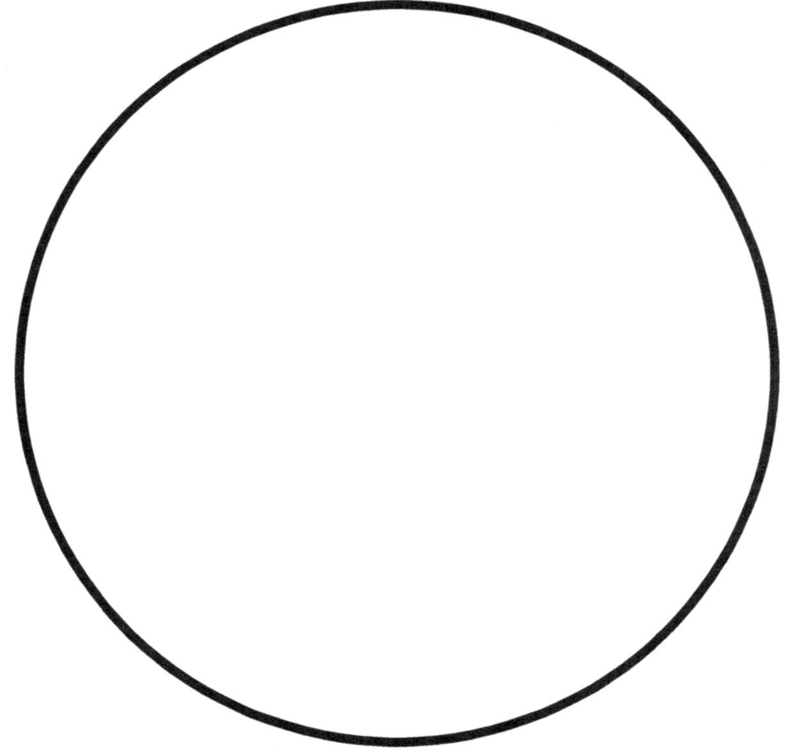

## SIMPLE COLUMNAR EPITHELIUM   (Small Intestine)

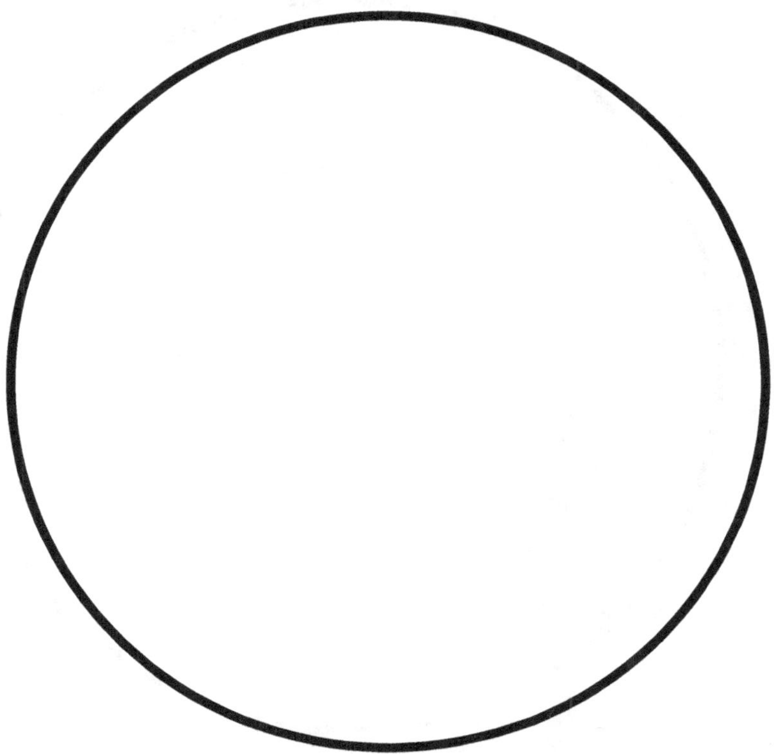

## PSEUDO STRATIFIED EPITHELIUM (Trachea)

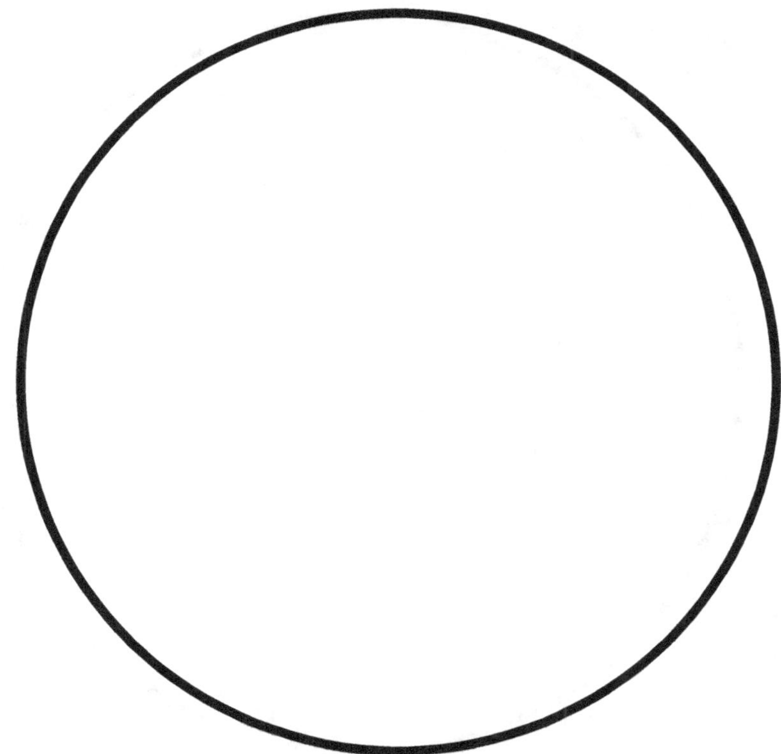

## TRANSITIONAL EPITHELIUM

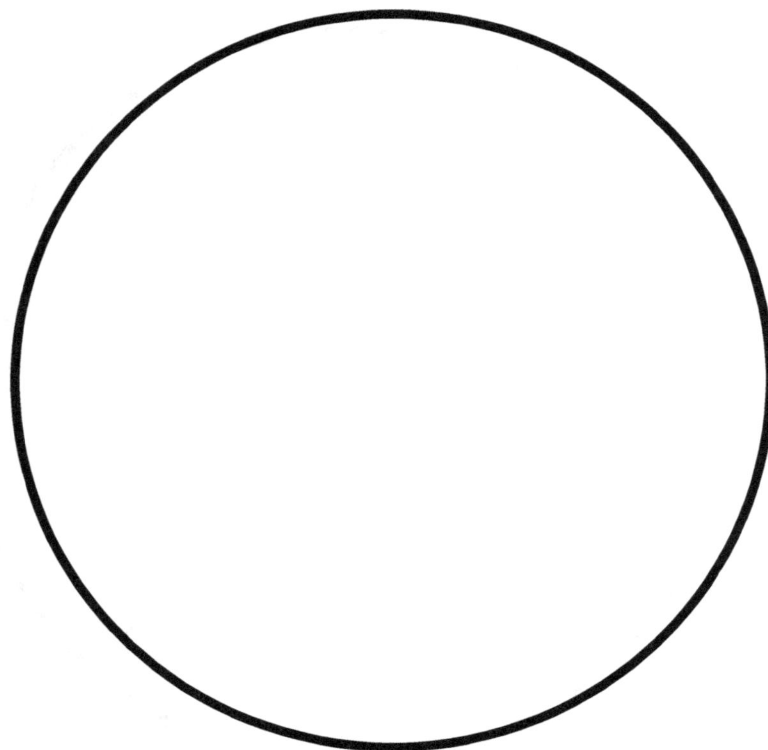

## STRATIFIED SQUAMOUS EPITHELIUM(Moist)

### (Oesophagus)

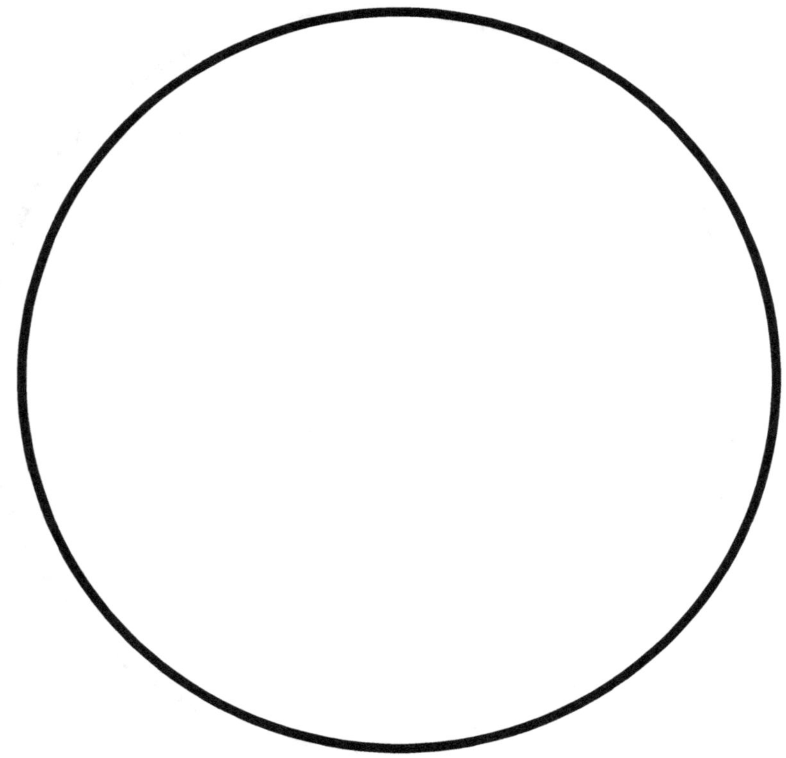

## STRTIFIED SQUAMOUS EPITHELIUM (Dry - Skin)

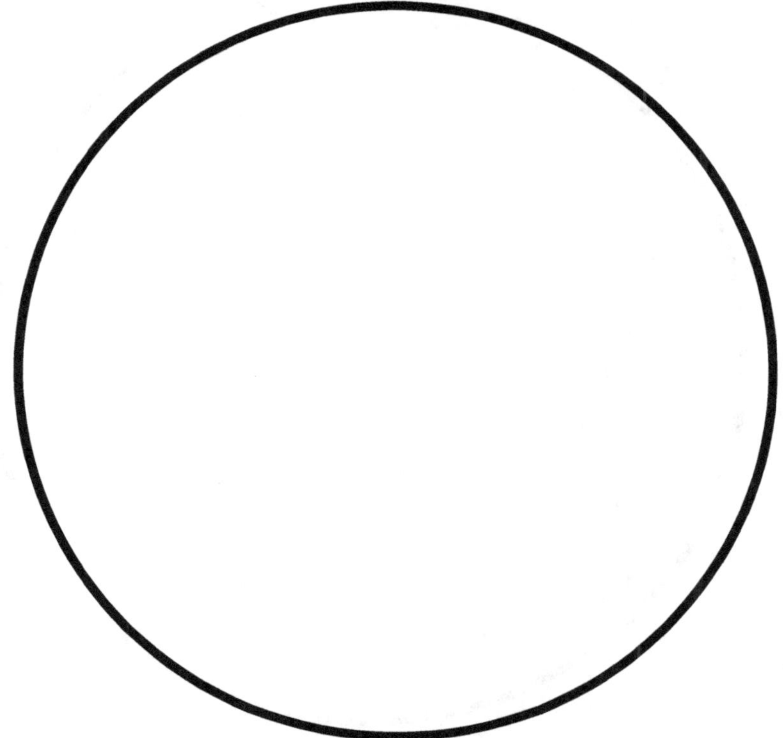

## STRATIFIED CUBOIDAL EPITHELIUM

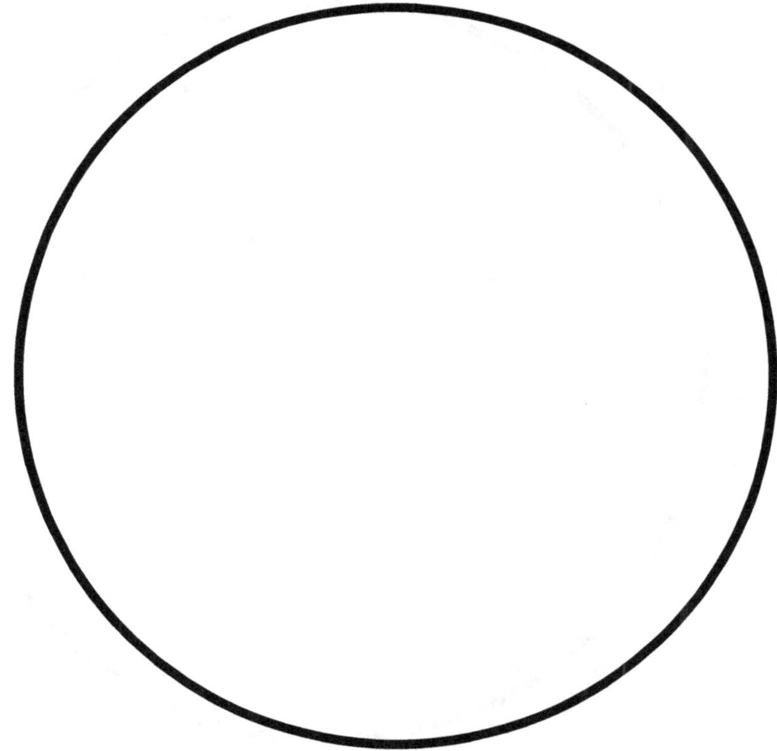

## STRATIFIED COLUMNAR EPITHELIUM

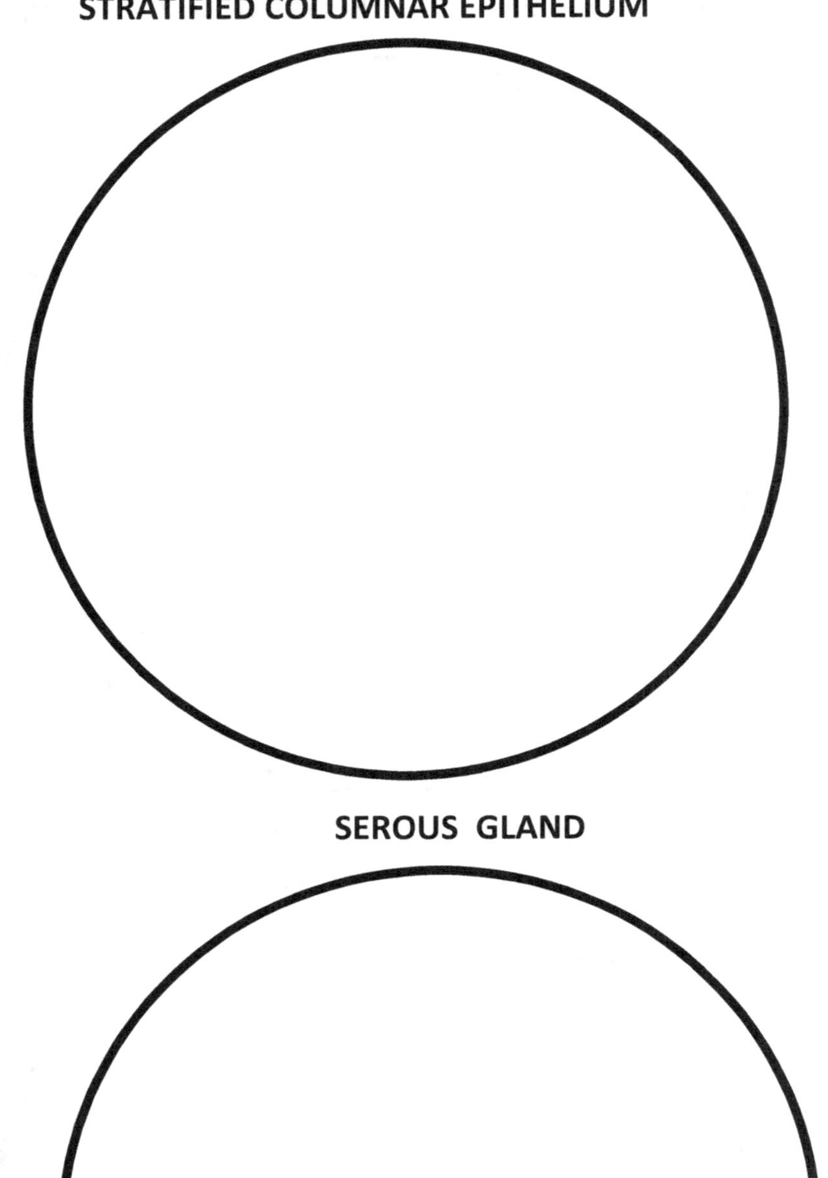

## SEROUS  GLAND

## MUCOUS  GLAND

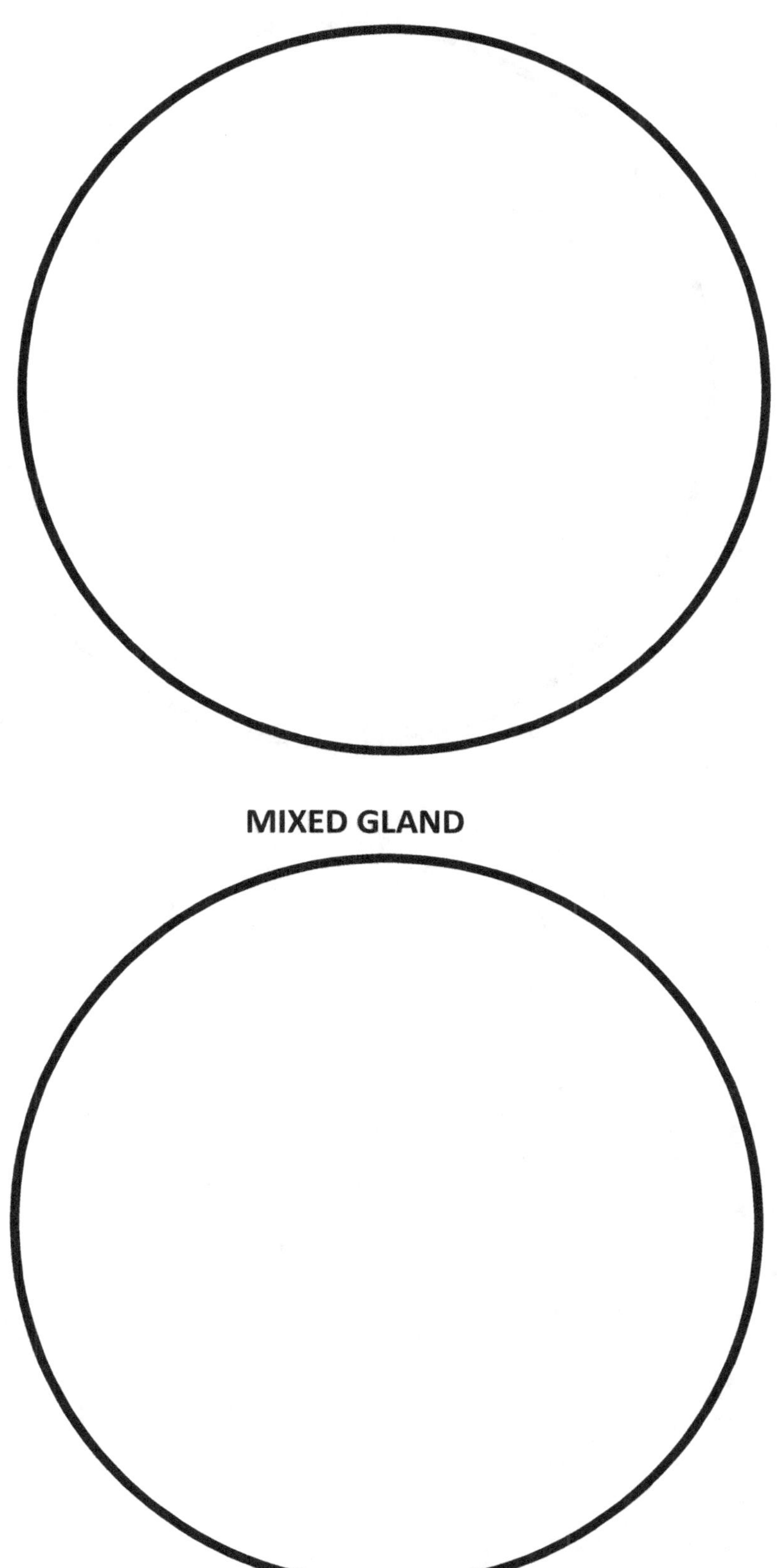

## MIXED GLAND

## GOBLET CELL (Large Intestine)

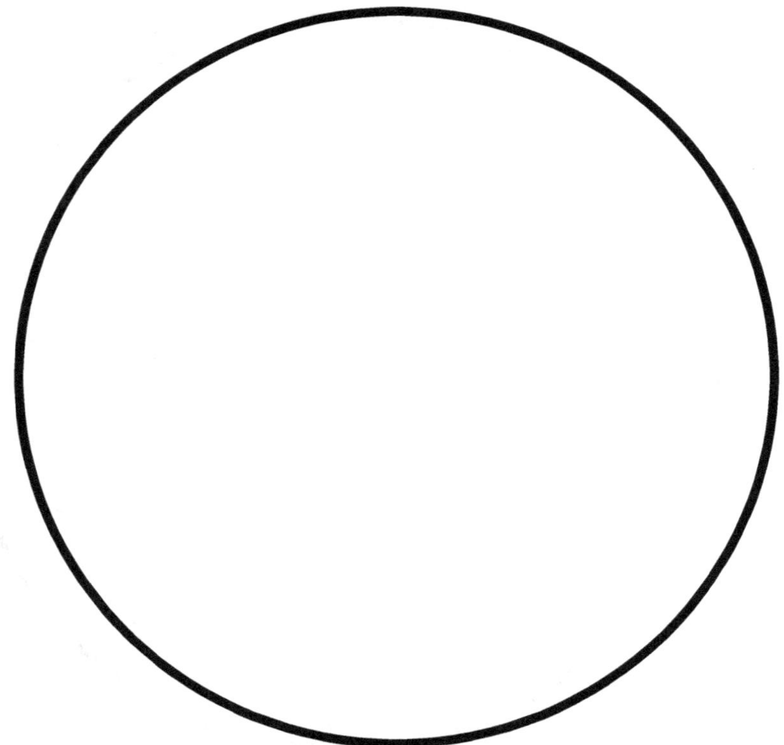

# CHAPTER NO. 4.  CONNECTIVE TISSUE

**Definition:-**It is the supporting framework, and packing material for functionally active organs of body. It is a binding; connecting tissue which holds structures together e.g. Neurovascular bundles; muscle fibres are hold together by loose connective tissue. Skin is firmly attached to deeper structure by connective tissue.

## CLASSIFICATION OF CONNECTIVE TISSUE

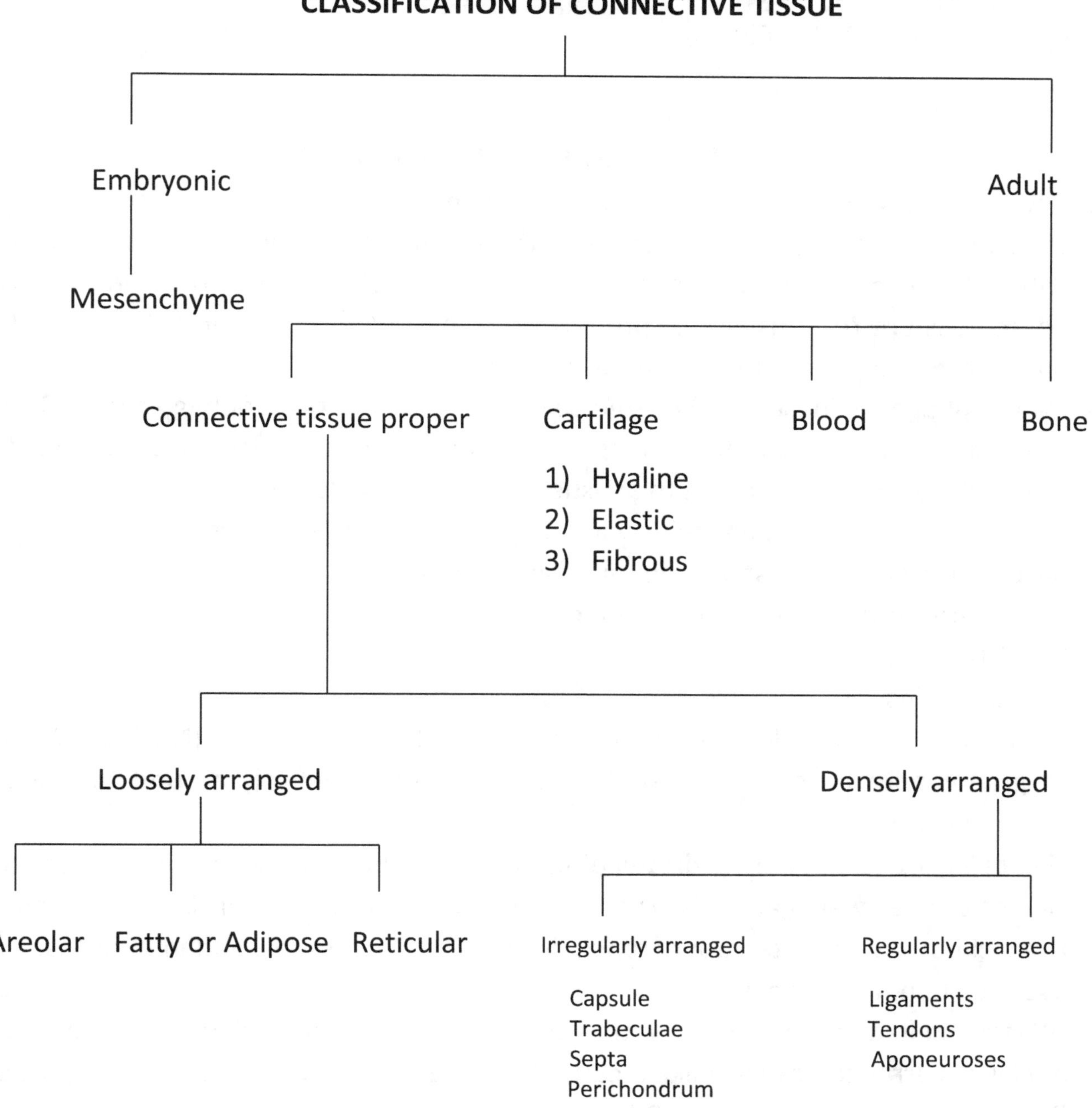


All the connective tissues are composed of the following constituents.

**1. CELLS**
1) Fibroblast
2) Macrophage
3) Mast cells
4) Plasma cells
5) Fat cells
6) Different W.B Cs of blood

**2.Intercellular Substance**

**Fibers**
1) Collagen fibers
2) Elastic fibers
3) Recticularfibers

**Amorphous Substances** consist of protein and polysaccharide complexes as
a) Chondroitin sulphate
b) Hyluronicacides

## SOME DETAILS OF THE CELL

1) **Fibroblast cell-** Flattened, irregular cells, having branching process, branches join to form network. In section of tissue of the fibroblast appears spindle shaped cell with a fusiform body and tapering ends. Nucleus is rod like in the central part. These cells are responsible for production of elastic and collagen fibre, and take part in repair of tissue, forming a fibrous scar.

2) **Macrophages –** These are the large cells, having properties of phagocytosis. They are stained by intravital staining e.g. Kupffer cells in the liver sinusoids. Macrophages may be fixed in the tissue or may be wandering.

3) **Mast cells-** small round cells with large round nucleus. Cytoplasm contains basophilic granules. Responsible for production of
a) Heparin- prevents clotting of blood.
b) Histamine.
c) Serotonins.
   Mast cells show Meta chromatic staining with Toludine blue (Nucleus blue & granules in the cytoplasm red). They are seen frequently around the blood vessels.

4) **Fat cells-** are large round cells full of fat in the cytoplasm. Nucleus pressed on the side of the cell wall. Fat is dissolved in xylol during processing of tissue and hence the cell has a vacuolated appearance, in H & E Stained slides. Sudan III or black is used to stain fat specially.

5) **Plasma cell-** are large cells with, large oval or round nucleus, chromatin of nucleus is arranged radially like a cart wheel. Nucleus usually eccentrically placed. Plasma cell represents mature B-lymphocyte.

6) **Leucocytes**- lymphocytes; eosinophils and sometime monocytes may be seen in connective tissue.

7) **Pigment cell**- are called chromatophores. They contain black pigment melanin. They are present in the connective tissue of the skin; choroid and iris of the eye. Pigment cells are derived from neural crest.

## FIBERS

i) **Collagen fibres**- long white fibres found in bundles with wavy appearance without any branch. Boiling of the fibres in water yield gelatine. They are stained pink with eosin. Each collagen fibre consists of fibrils; and each fibril consists of finer, fibrils which shows cross striations in electron microscopy. Collagen fibre consist of Tropocollagen protein. The amino acid content of the fibre varies with different type of collagen Fibres. Tropocollagen is laid down by the fibroblasts. Collagen fibers resist considerable tensile forces without stretching themselves.

ii) **Elastic fibres**-  are very fine, thin, single fibres with cured ends. They form a network and not bundles. Boiling, acids and alkalis have no effect on them, but are destroyed by enzymes. Orcein is the special stain for these fibres. It consists of protein called elastin. They can be stretched and regain original length.

iii) **Reticular fibres**-found mainly in bone marrow; lymphoid tissue, liver. These are very fine branching fibres. They support glandular tissue and form basement membrane. They are stained black with silver impregnation method. They have same chemical structure as collagen fibres and show striations. But they differ-

a) Reticular fibres are much finer. b) Form a network(not bundles). Reticular fibers are mainly supportive to loose cells of glandular organs like liver, spleen, lymph nodes etc. They are seen in capsule, trabeculae, septa and form a reticular network for loose cells. They are argyrophilic fibres having affinity for silver dyes.

**Mesenchyme**- This is embryonic connective tissue and consists of small cells with branching processes, which join to form a network. The cells are undifferentiated and can form any type of connective tissue cell. Umbilical cord, mesenchymal cells are seen holding the foetal blood vessels.

## TENDON:

Tendon offers a great resistance to pulling force of muscle. Fibres are arranged in thick bundles, which have a wary appearance. Fibroblasts (Tendon cells) are only seen in between fibre bundles. The collagen fibres run parallel, in the tendon.

## PRACTICAL HINTS:

1) **Slide of umbilical cord-** look for the stellate cells scattered all over. Their processes join each other and form network. Inter-cellular substance is not seen, as same is dissolved in water during processing. Foetal blood vessels (who arteries and one vein) are seen in the centre.

2) **Loose areolar tissue-** If slide is stained with H & E Stain, elastic fibres are stain deep pink, and collagen fibres faint pink colour. Fibroblasts are seen but their walls are not so clearly visible. Collagen fibres in wavy pink bundles; elastic fibres are single and branching.

3) **Adipose tissue-** (Slide stained with H&E) Note the vacuolated appearance of the cell and the nucleus pressed on the cell wall; flattened. Fat is removed during processing. Hence vacuolated appearance.

4) **Tendon-** (Stained with H&E- T.S.) Note the cut end of the collagen fibres. The darkly stained wing like nuclei of tendon cells in centre.

5) **Reticular Tissue-** looks for the darkly stained jet black fine fibrils, forming a network. Lymphocytes and other cells seen packed up in the reticular network.

### QUESTION:

1) Enumerate the functions of areolar tissue?
2) What is the action of the week Acetic Acid on the connective tissue fibres?
3) Why do you see vacuolated appearance of fat cells in stained paraffin section of fatty tissue?
4) Name the stains used for fatty cells?
5) What is Wharton's jelly? What type of tissue it is? Do you find it in adult tissue?
6) Give the staining reaction of reticular fibres? Where do you find these fibres?
7) What is the arrangement of white fibres in tendons?

## AREOLAER TISSUE

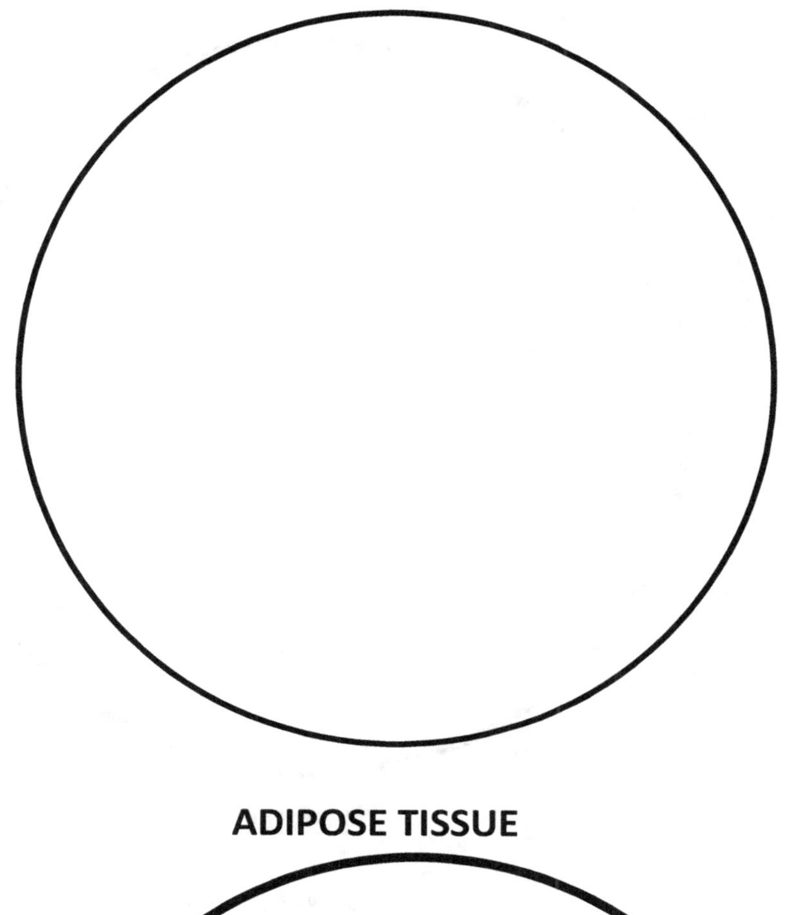

## ADIPOSE TISSUE

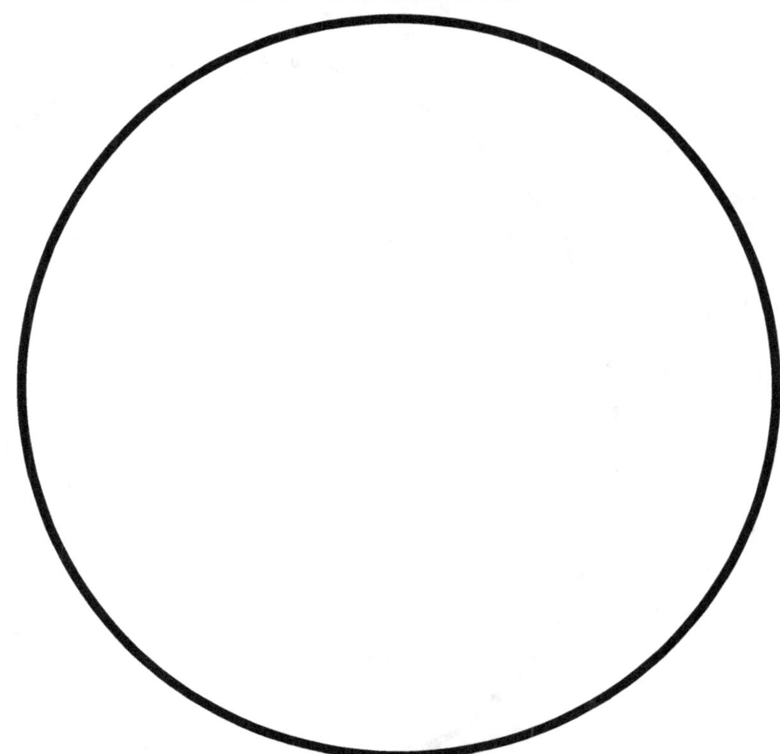

## RETICULAR TISSUE (Silver Nitrate Stain)

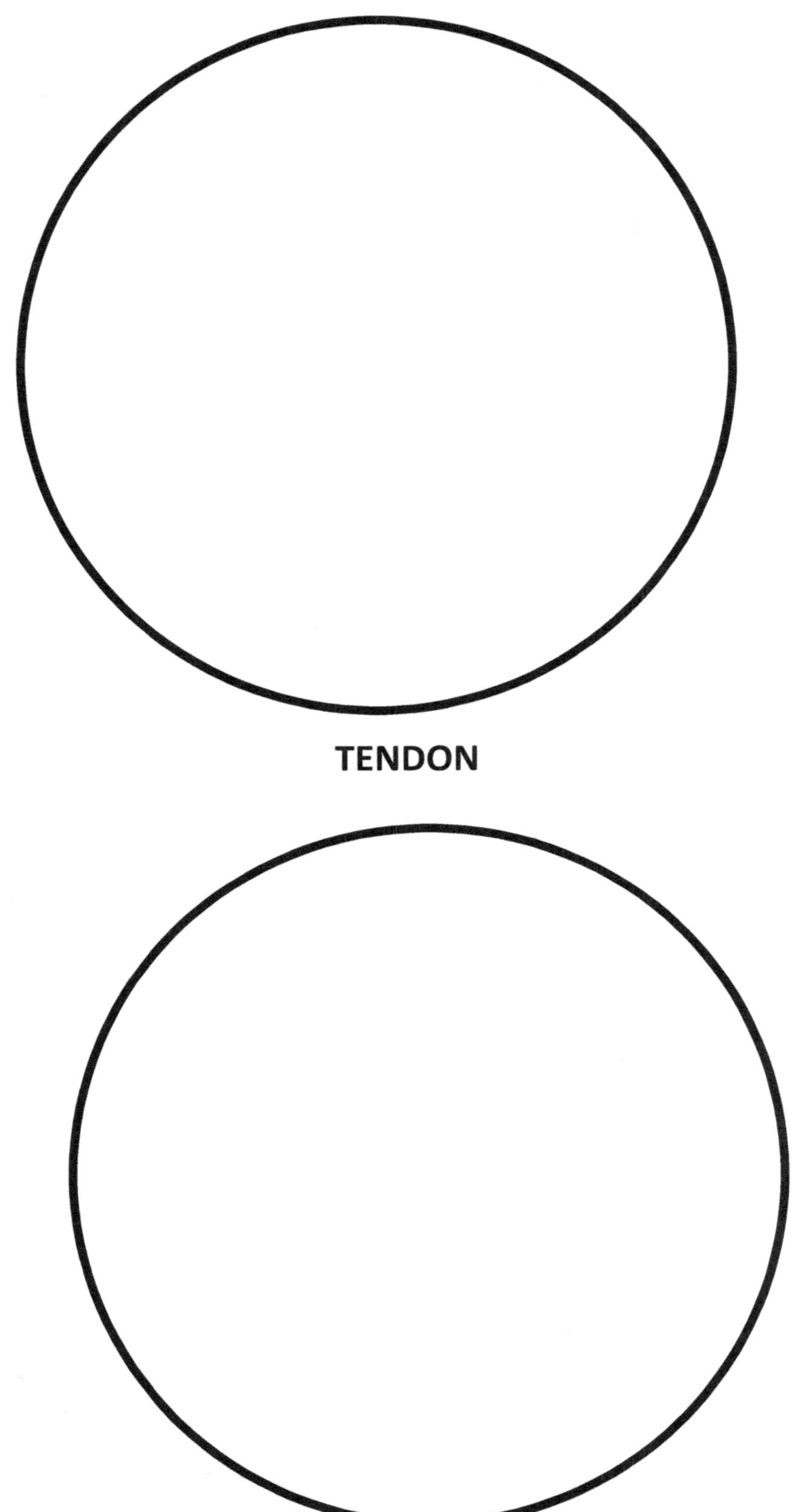

**TENDON**

## MUCOID TISSUE (Umbilical cord)

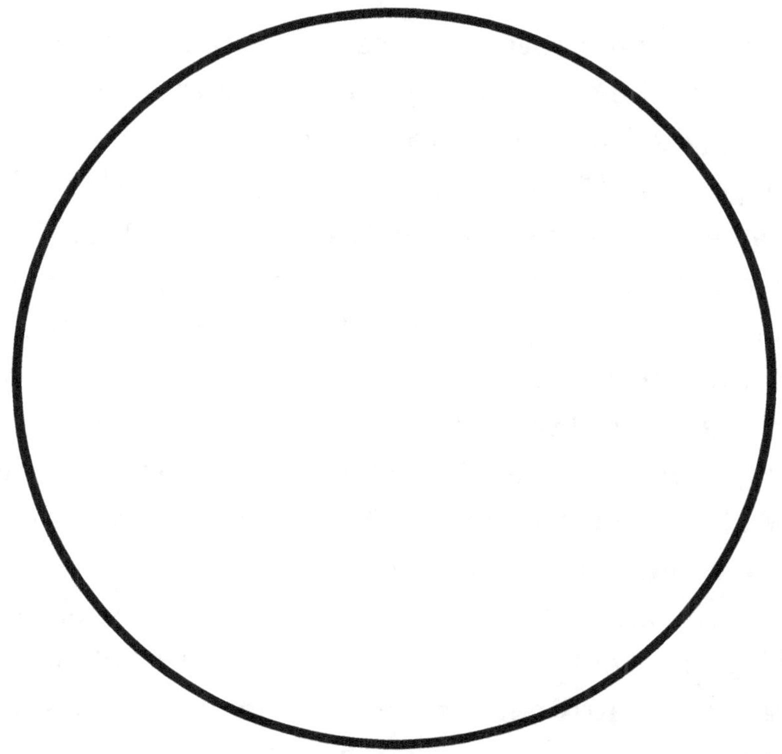

# Chapter 5.   CARTILAGE

This special connective tissue can with stand great pressure and tension; and is made up of the cells and inter cellular substances and fibres. Cartilage is quite firm and gives some rigidity to the structure.

**Cartilage cells (Chondrocytes)-** are spherical or oval in shape. Occurs singly (young cells) or in groups (dividing cells) of 2, 4, 6, 8 with their flattened surfaces opposing each other. The cells contain lot of glycogen and fat, which gives the cell vacuolated appearance. The grouping of cartilage cells is due to mitoses and internal growth.

**Matrix-** appears homogeneous with lacunae (spaces) in it. Spaces are occupied by the chondrocytes. Matrix is stiff gelatinous ground substances with a fine network of collagen fibres. Chemically it is chondro-muco-protiens; a complex of mucoprotein and chondroitin sulphate.

The matrix near the lacuna is youngest and basophilic. The basophilia is because of high concentration of acidic chondroitin sulphate and few collagen fibres. The general matrix between lacunae appears more eosinophilic, because of less of chondroitin sulphate and more collagen fibres.

**Fibres-** fibres are present in the matrix. Depending upon the type of fibre present in the matrix the cartilage is classified.

**Classifications-** classified according to the predominance of structural element-

1)   **Cellular cartilage-** is not a human tissue eg, slide of pinna of Rabbit. Cells present predominantly and less of intercellular substance.

2)   **White fibrocartilage-**  Perichondrium is absent. Matrix is studded with white collagen fibres. Few cells are present in lacunae with small amount of amorphous matrix surrounding. Seen at the junction of tendon with bone at the periosteum. Interverebvral discuses are best example of fibracartilage. This cartilage has great tensile strength and elasticity.

3)   **Elastic cartilage-**  Perichondrium is present. Matrix is studded with elastic fibres forming felt work. Cells are seen in capsule in matrix which is non homogeneous like Hyaline cartilage because of presence of elastic fibre network. Elastic cartilage is very flexible and regains original shape easily. It is

present where elasticity & firmness is required.  E.g pinna of ear; lateral part of external acoustic meatus, and medial part of auditory tube; epiglottis.

   **4)   Hyaline cartilage-** It is called hyaline because it appears transparent. Matrix is homogeneous. Perichondrium is present. Cells are present in lacunae. Cells are young singly present near the (chondroblast) outer layer consists of collagen fibres. The chonroblast layer produces the chondrocytes which migrate to the central region of the cartilage.

   **Perichondrium-** is fibrous covering of cartilage. Innermost layer is made up of flattened cells (chondroblasts). Outer layer consists of collagen fibres. The chondroblast layer produces the chondrocytes which migrate to the central region of the cartilage.

   **Nutrition of cartilage-** it is supplied through the inner cellular matrix by diffusion as the cartilage is devoid of blood vessels and nerve fibres. Blood vessels are present in perichondrium.

## PRACTICAL HINTS

   1)   **Slide of Hyaline cartilage-** (Trache H & E stain) look for outmost fibrous covering (Perichordrium) made up of collagen fibres, its inner layer made up of flattened cells. Look for the scattered cartilage cells, either single or in groups. Note vacuolated appearance (Lacunce) of matrix seen as clear empty spaces. Cell bodies seen inside the lacunae. Nuclei stained deep. Matrix is stained pinkish (Homogenous mass). The matrix appears homogeneous as refractive index of collagen fibres and matrix is same.

   2)   **Slide of white fibro cartilage-** junction of tendon with bone or intervertebral disk. White fibres predominate, having pink colour. Note the parallel arrangement of fibres with cartilage cells in between the fibres. There is absence of perichondrium. The cells (chondrocytes) are few.

   3)   **Slide of elastic cartilage-** (Epiglottis; H & E stain). Note the perichondrium, inside the perichondrium find the network of elastic fibres enclosing the single, large cartilage cells.

**QUESTION:**

1) Name the three varieties of cartilage? Where are they found?
2) What is perichondrium? In which cartilage it is absent?
3) What is the function of perichondrium?
4) Why the fibres are not visualised in hyaline cartilage?

## HYALINE CARTILAGE (Trachea)

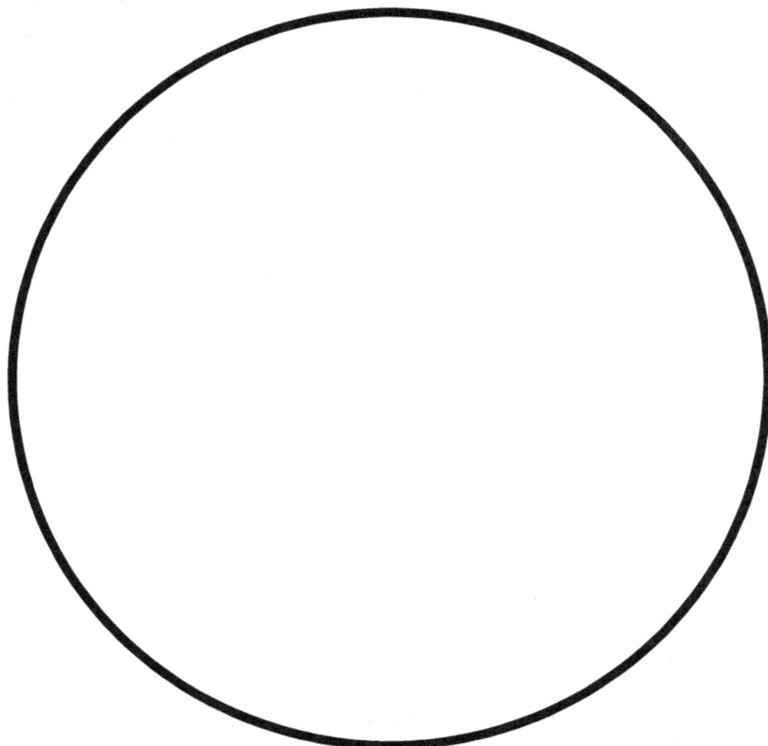

## YELLOW ELASTIC CARTILAGE (Epiglottis)

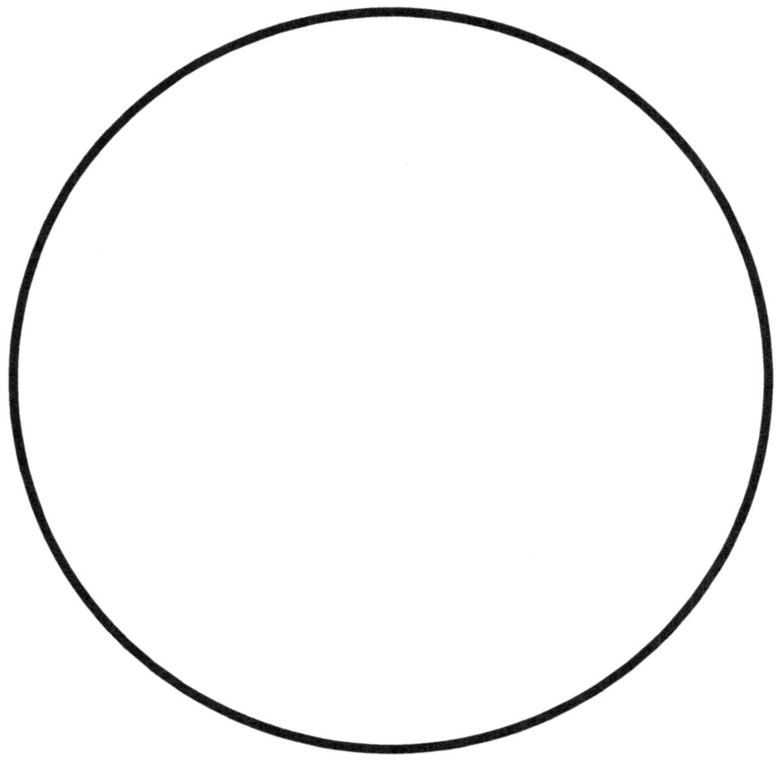

## WHITE FIBROCARTILAGE

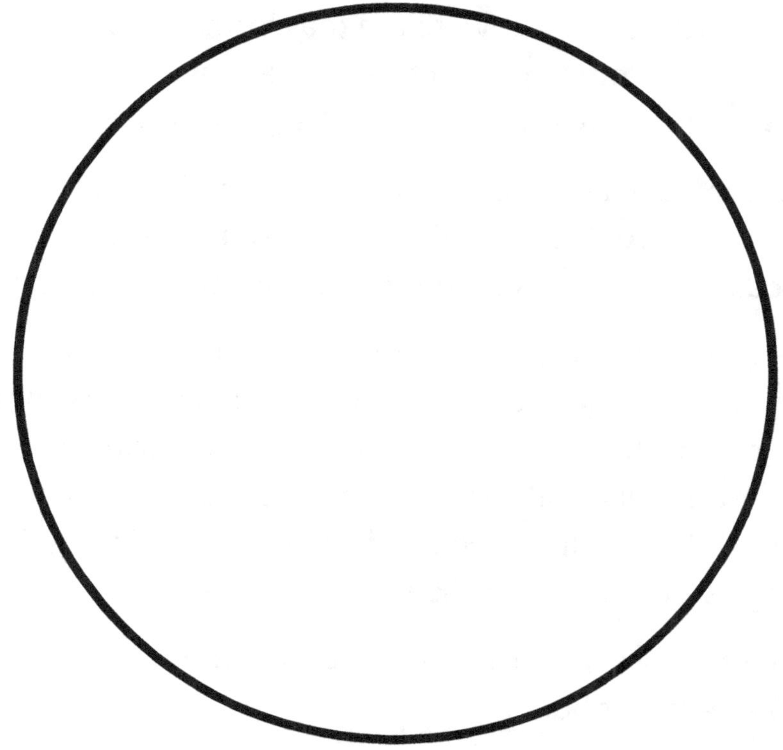

# Chapter 6.   BONE

It is the hardest connective tissue that forms the skeleton, giving support to the body structure. Like other connective tissue it is made up of cells; fibres and ground substances which contain inorganic salts and calcium.

**Spongy Bone & Compact Bone-** spongy bone formed by trabeculae; arranged in a manner corresponding to the direction of maximum pressure and tension. It is present at the ends of long bones covered by a thin layer of compact bone.

**Compact bone –** forms the outer layer of the bone. It is most compact in shaft of the long bone. Bony lamellae are compactly arranged. The bone has lacunae inside it giving space for osteocytes. The long vertical canals (Haversian) which anastomose with each other externally and inside with medullary cavity by minute horizontal canals (Volkmann's). Volkmann's canals are not surrounded by bony lamellae while Haversian canal are surrounded lamellae.

**Structure of bone-**microscopic structure of both spongy bone and compact bone is basically similar i.e. lamellar bone.

A)   **Periosteum-** it covers the bone. It has two layers.
 1)  Outer Fibrous layer composed of collagen fibres and few elastic fibres with numerous blood vessels. **Sharpey's Fibres** are collagen fibres of periosteum penetrating the bone tissue underneath up to outer circumferential lamellae and interstitial lamellae. These fibres are mainly present in large numbers at the insertion of tendon with bone. Sharpey's fibres fix the periosteum to the bone as they are embedded in matrix.
 2)  Inner osteogenic layer composed of flattened cells in loose connective tissue with bone forming actively. Osteogenic cells are responsible for bone growth and repair.

B)   **Endosteum-** covers the internal surface of the bone. It has the same component as the periosteum and nearly same structure, but it is much thinner and does not have two layers.

**Functions of periosteum & Endosteum-** the blood vessels present in the connective tissue of periosteum and endosteum penetrate the bone through canals called Volkmann's canals and supply branches to Haversian system.

a) Supply nourishment to bony tissue.

b) Supply of new osteoblasts for growth and repair.

## Structural elements of bone.

1) **Bone cells.**   2) **Ground substance.**  3) **Fibres.**

1) **Bone cells:**
   - ➢ **Osteoblast-** are the large bone forming cells. Once the bone is formed they are imprisoned in the matrix & called as osteocytes. Cytoplasmic processes are formed for the nourishment of the bone cells as the matrix is calcified and nourishment cannot go by diffusion through matrix to the bone cells like the cartilage cells. Osteocytes are concentrically arranged around the Haversian canal with inter posing matrix which thus forms lamellae. The cytoplasmic process of the osteocytes unite with each other and then to the Haversian canal.
   - ➢ **Osteoclasts-**  These are present on endosteal surface of the bone. It is a large motile multinucleated cell. It absorbs the bone under the influence of parathormone.

2) **Matrix-** consists of  a) Mucopolysaccharide with chondroitin sulphate &

b) Collagen fibres. Both (a&b) form the organic portion of matrix.

c) **Inorganic salts-** Forms 50% of matrix. Calcium and phosphorus form hydroxyapatite crystals. They are elongated needle like structures present alongside the collagen fibres; thus giving strength to the bone.

3) **Fibres** – Large number of collagen fibres are present in matrix giving it elasticity.

**Haversian system-** (unit of bone) The osteon consists of a centrally located system of blood vessel, nerves & connective tissue in the Haversian canal; surrounded by concentrically arranged lamellae of collagen fibres with cementing substance. Osteocytes are found in lacunae between the lamellae. Haversian bone system is mainly found in the compact bone of diaphysis. The vertical Haversian canals containing blood vessels are connected to periosteum and narrow cavity by the horizontally running Volkmann's canals. The Volkmann's canals do not have lamellae; on the other hand they traverse the lamellae. They carry blood vessels from perichondrium.

Haversian system is formed by deposition of lamellae by osteoblasts from periphery towards the canal. There is growth and destruction and rebuilding going on continuously in children as well as in adults. Net Haversian systems are thus formed.

1) **Circumferential lamellae-** Lamellae parallel to the surface present just deep to periosteum and endosteum are circumferential lamellae.
2) **Haversian lamellae-** Lamellae present surrounding the Halverson canals. Each lamella consists of collagen fibres matrix and inorganic salts deposited in it. Between lamellae the osteocytes are present in lacunae.
3) **Interstitial lamellae-**During the formation of new Haversian system older Haversian lamellae are destroyed and parts of these are left out. They are called interstitial lamellae.

## Ossification of Bones

Bone is formed either in a membrane or in a cartilage.
Intramembrenous condensation of mesenchymal cells change into osteoblast which lay down matrix. Side by side remodelling of bone is done by osteoblast cells.

### INTRA CARTILAGENOUS (ENDOCHONDRAL)

Intra-membranous classification is observed in skull cap bones. Intra-cartilagenous classification is seen with long bones. Small cartilage models of the long bone are formed from mesenchyme. Various zones are seen in the developing bone (cartilage model).

**Know about developing Bones (Ends of long bones)**

1)   Mesenchymal cells assemble together and form one mass.
2)   These cells change into cartilage cells (cartilage models is formed) with fibrous covering of perichondrium.
3)   Cartilage cells enlarge, arrange, in parallel rows along the long axis of bone. These are degenerating and hypertrophied cells containing much glycogen.
4)   Matrix surrounding the enlarged cells to calcify. Thus cartilage cells do not get nourishment by diffusion.

5) Enlarged cartilage cells die, degenerate and get absorbed by osteoblasts.

6) At the same time changes are going on the perichondrium and a layer of flattened oval cells is formed (osteoblasts).

7) Periosteal bud is formed by projection of fibres, osteoblasts, osteoclasts and blood vessels on the inner surface of periosteum. Blood vessels pierce the collar bone that is formed at the periphery, beneath the periosteum and enter the cartilage. Cells and blood vessels occupy the empty spaces.

8) Osteoclasts engulf the dead cartilage cells.

9) Osteoblast lay down calcified concentric lamellae round about the Haversian canals which are formed by growing blood vessel; upwards and downwards from the centre of ossifying occupy bone.

10) This bone formation is under the influence of various factors-

   a) Nutrition  b) Vit D.   c) calcium and proteins.

   d) hormones- growth hormones; paratharmone; calcitonin, Oestrogen, testosterone.

# PRACTICAL HINTS

1) **Slide of ground bone(T-S)**  see the central yellowish dark Haversian canal surrounded by concentric lamellae. Dark coloured oval or round lacunae are seen in between the lamellae. Hairs like dark canaliculi arising from these lacunae are seen forming network.

2) **Slid of ground bone(L-S)** the same structure as in T.S except the canals are cut longitudinally or obliquely. Lacunae are arranged parallel to Haversian canals.

3) **Decalcified bones (T.S. H & E).** Haversian canal seen as central circular empty spot. Lacunae are arranged concentrically around the canals. Decalcified bony matrix looks as homogenous pink stained mass.

4) **Decalcified bone (L.S. H&E)** seen as in T.S but canal are cut obliquely and longitudinally. Lacunae are arranged parallel to Haversian canal.

5) **Developing Bone (H & E)** – See the epiphyseal zone. See the fibrous perichondrium and its inner layer of osteoblast cells. Move the slide till you come across the most evident structure of regularly arranged rows of cartilage cells. Focus your attention at this sport. Note the shape of the cartilage is like the army soldiers standing in rows one behind the other.

   At the developing end you will see cartilage cells and where the bone is just forming bigger degeneration of cells. Where the bone is formed, irregular masses of bone are seen. Look for big spaces filled with blood cells. This is future bone marrow.

   Gliant cells (osteoclasts are seen in the irregular margins), Howship's Lacunae of the bony plates & osteoblasts are seen scattered throughout the matrix.

## COMPACT BONE (T.S)

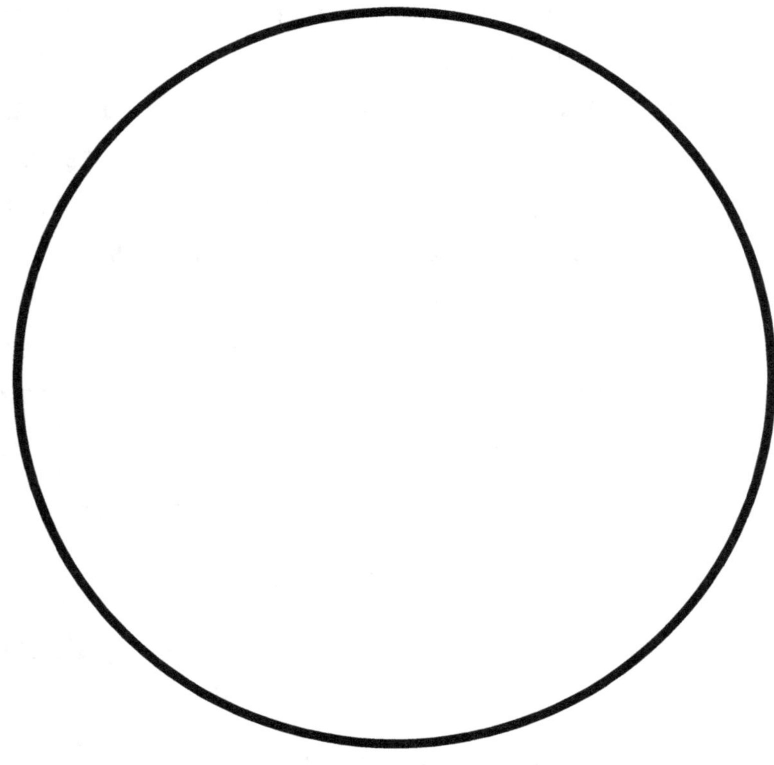

## COMPACT BONE (L.S)

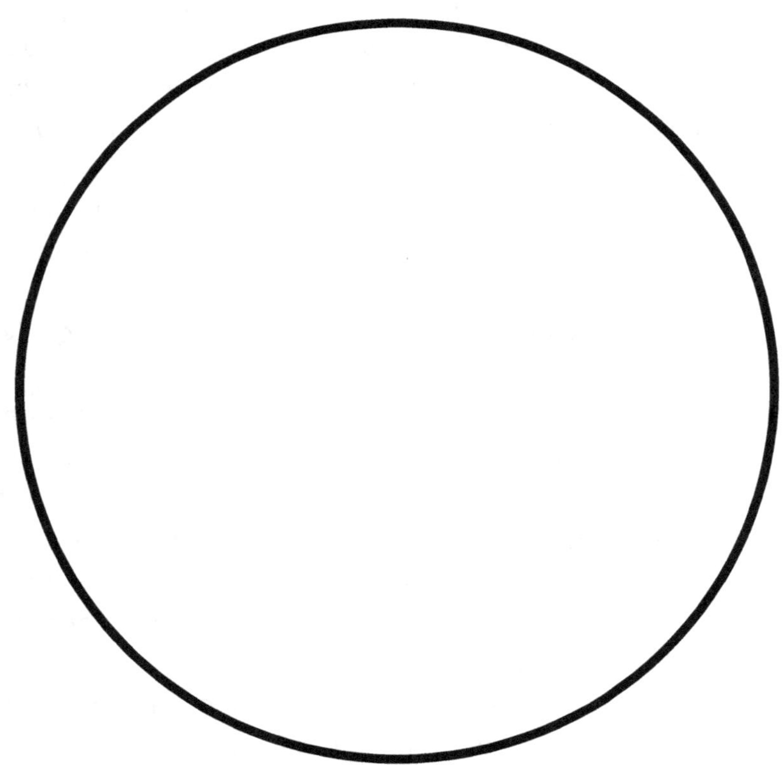

## DEVELOPING BONE

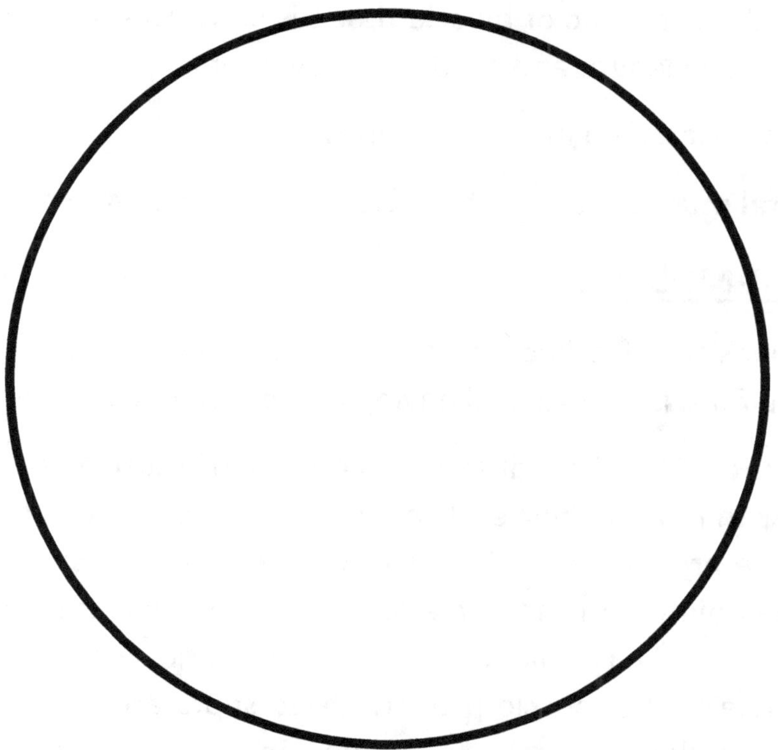

# CHAPTER 7. MUSCLE TISSUE

The characteristic of muscle tissue is contraction. By this property, the muscle cell shortens in length and produces movement.

Muscles are classified in to three types-

**1. Skeletal muscle, 2. Smooth muscle & 3. Cardiac muscle**

## 1. <u>SKELETAL MUSCLE</u>:

Muscle consists of cylindrical cell. Length may vary, long as in Sartorius muscle. Each muscle fibre is a single cell having number of nuclei along its length.

**STRUCTURE:** The skeletal muscle consists of muscles cells which are very much elongated with multiple nuclei. The muscle cells or myocytes form a thick bundle (the whole muscle proper) which is covered by connective tissue sheet called epimysium. Through the epimysium the nerve and blood vessels enter the muscles to supply the muscle tissue. The nerve blood vessels travel via fibrous septa which separate smaller muscle bundle in the muscle proper. These septa are call perimysium as they cover the muscle bundles. Each muscle bundle consists of number of muscle cells; each cell covered by its own sheath of connective tissue, called endomysium. A muscle cell is called fibre as it is long. Each muscle fibre has plasma membrane (Sarcolemma) and cytoplasm (Sacrcoplasm). In the sarcoplasm, there are myofibrils.

Each myofibril has a number of myofilaments. Myofibrils have alternate dark and light bands. Positions of these bands in one fibril correspond exactly with other fibrils. This gives the muscle a striated appearance. In between the myofibrils in the sarcoplasm, there are number of mitochondria, endoplasmic reticulum, glycogen etc. Nuclei are pushed to the periphery of the muscle fibre by the fibrils. Perinuclear golgi apparatus etc. are present.

Dark areas on myofibril are 'A' bands (Anisotropic) and light areas are 'I' bands (Isotropic). Z line is dark line in light band I. There is a light band in middle of dark band A called as H band. Area between two adjacent Z line is called as Sarcomere which is functional unit of skeletal muscle. M line is present in centre of sarcomere (Mid line of H band).

Myofilaments consist of finely beaded chain of protein material know as actin and myosin. Dark band and light band depend on refractile nature of the material.

**Some details of Myofilament:**

In a muscle fibre (cell) there are number of myofibrils. Each myofibril has number of myofilaments.

**Myofilaments are of two types:**

1)  **Actin and**
2)  **Myosin**
    a)  Myosin filaments are thicker and occupy the whole length of Dark Band.
    b)  Actin filaments are much thinner and start from the Z line and enter the dark band in between the myosin filaments where they inter digitate with myosin filaments. These actin filaments do not extend throughout the dark band, but fall short in centre of dark band, so that there is a gap in between these filaments. This is the reason for the line (Hensen's line) in dark band. When muscle contracts, the Henson's band get obliterated as the ends of actin filaments approach each other and fill the gap.

## BLOOD VESSELS :

Form a plexus in the epimysium and capillary plexus in the endomysium. Lymphatic plexus is also present in epimysium & perimysium.

## RED AND WHITE MUSCLE:

**RED MUSCLE-** contains large amount of pigment called myoglobin, hence red in colour. Larger quantity of glycogen and oxidative enzymes with abundant elongated mitochondria are present in red muscle fibre. This muscle contracts slowly but the contraction is well sustained. Hence the postural muscles are made of Red muscle fibres.

**White muscle-** Myoglobin is much less in amount; contraction is strong and quick but not well sustained e.g. muscles of fingers & eye ball. In human a mixture of both types is seen in the skeletal muscles.

## 2. <u>CARDIAC MUSCLE:</u>

Like skeletal muscle it shows striations. But appearance in the microscope is different and the muscle has its own rhythm of contraction. It is involuntary. The cardiac muscle consists of cells called myocytes. Each cell is a small compared to skeletal muscle. The cell shows branching pattern. Adjacent myocytes show peculiar darkly stained discs between them called the intercalated discs as seen in the light microscope. With EM each disc appears to be due to junctional complexes between the cells. The myocytes are separated by loose connective tissue containing blood vessel and nerves. Each myocyte shows a round vesicular nucleus in the central region and faint striations in the peripheral part of the cell. The striations are due to Actin & Myosin (contractile proteins) in the myofibrils. In cardiac muscle sarcoplasm is more and myofibrils are less, hence striations are less prominent than as seen in skeletal muscle. Cardiac muscle contracts of its own. The pace maker is situated at SA node. The wave of contraction is carried by specialized muscle fibres called the conducting system of the heart (i.e. Purkinjee fibres). Motor end plates are not seen in cardiac muscle.

The contraction can be made stronger and speed stimulated by the autonomic nerves which supply the heart. Sympathetic nerves stimulate heart rate; parasympathetic decreases heart rate. The conducting system consists of SA Node, the bundle of His present in the interventricular septum, and its branches right and left, going to right and left ventricles.

## 3. <u>SMOOTH MUSCLE</u> –

Present in the walls of the hollow organs I.e. of GI tract; urinary tracts. Blood vessels, uterus etc; the cells are long spindle shaped with tapering ends. Nucleus is fusiform present in the central part of the cell. The cells show indistinct longitudinal striations but no transverse striations (no dark & light bands). The cell arrangement is peculiar i.e. the tapering end of one cells is against the thick central part of the other. The actin and myosin filaments are not regularly arranged as in skeletal muscle. Hence, no striations are seen in smooth muscle.

Smooth muscles have same type of connective tissue arrangement, the endomysium surrounding a single cell, perimysium surrounding the layer of muscle cells and epimysium. Smooth muscle is supplied by autonomic nerves. The parasympathetic & sympathetic nerves have opposite effect. Contraction of smooth muscle is slow but sustained. The density of blood vessels present in the smooth muscles is much less than in skeletal muscle. Parasympathetic contracts the wall and relaxes the sphincter and sympathetic nerve contracts the sphincter and relaxes the walls.

**Ultrastructure-** Each smooth muscle has plasma membrane & the longitudinal striations are due to delicate myofilaments. Each myofilament consists of protein actin and myosin but do not have an ordered arrangement as in skeletal muscle. Hence on banding pattern is seen, mitochondria golgi apparatus etc. are present.

# PRACTICAL HINTS

1) **Striated muscle (H & E Stain)-**note the thickness offibres and striations. Compare with involuntary and cardiac muscle fibres (thinner size). Striations are very well marked in striated muscle then in cardiac or smooth muscles. See the striations under high power after lowering the condenser to cut off light partially.
2) **T.S of striated muscle (H & E stain)** – fibres polygonal in shape in prepared slide. Fibres arranged in small groups. See nuclei dot like at the periphery of the muscle.
3) **L.S & T.S. plane muscle-** slides stained with H. & E. muscles fibres stained pink. Note the spindle shaped cells. Cellular margins not clearly seen. Nuclei are stained dark violet and are spindle shape centrally placed.
4) **Cardiac muscles (H & E stain)** – fibres are thin as compared to skeletal muscle fibres. Note situated in the centre of the cells. Striations faint peripherally.

**Questions:**
1) Why do you see striations in skeletal muscle?
2) What is contractile unit of striated muscle?
3) What are endomysium, perimysium and epimysium?
4) What is bundle of His? How is it formed?
5) If bundle of His is damaged. What will be the effect on the heart beats?
6) What are actin and myosin filaments? How are they arranged in sarcomere of skeletal muscles?

## STRIATED MUSCLE (L.S & T.S)

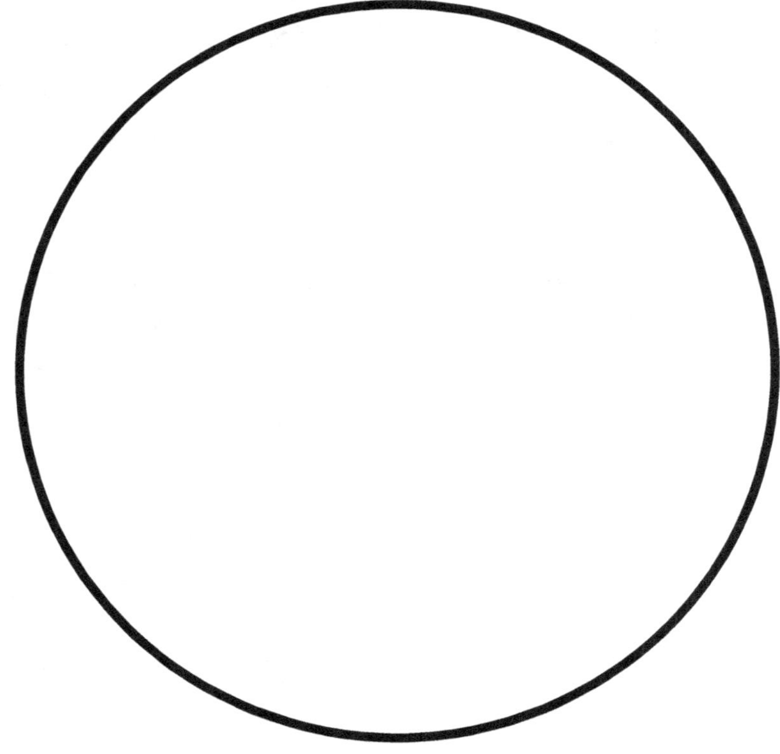

## SMOOTH MUSCLE (L.S & T.S)

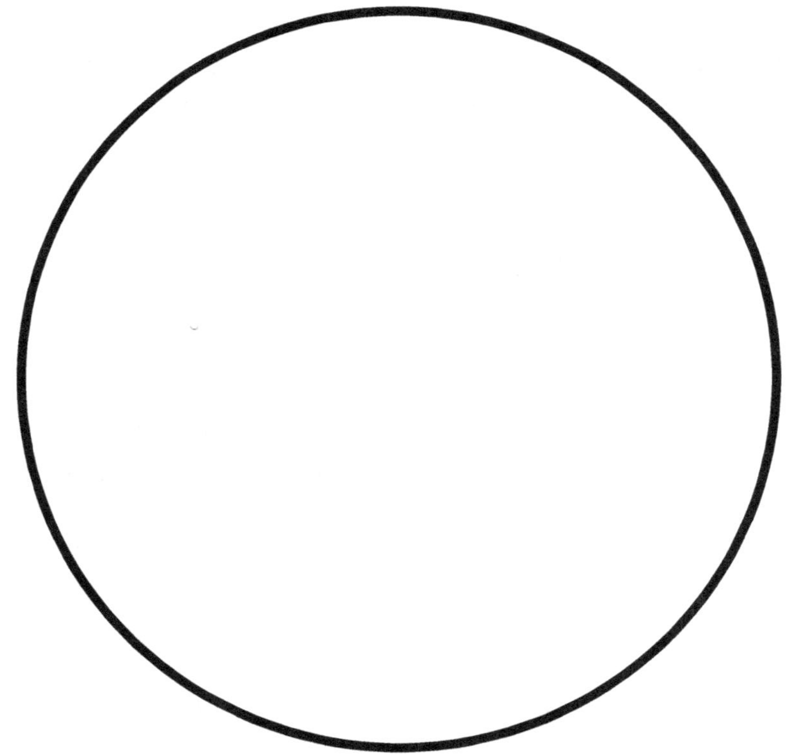

# CARDIAC MUSCLE

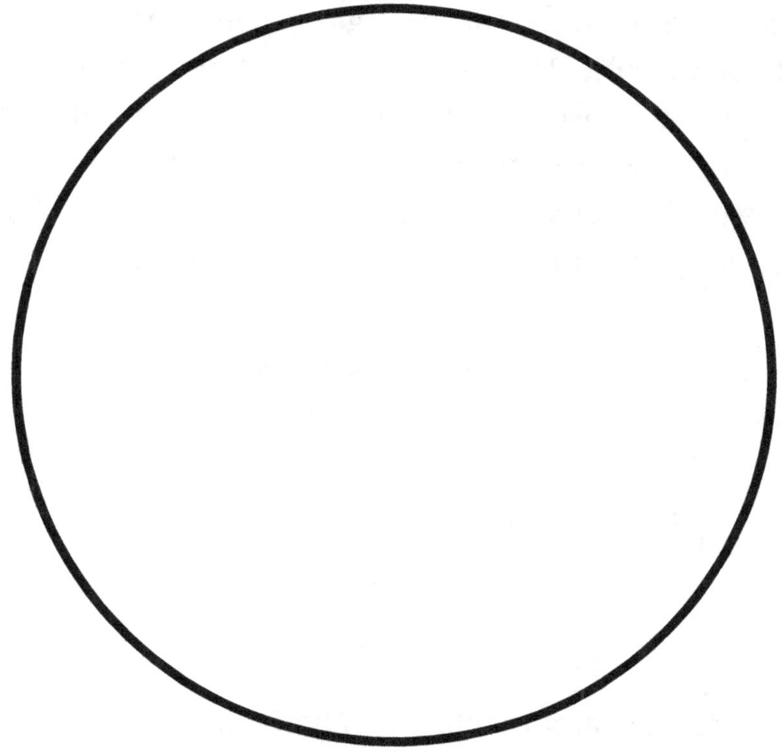

# CHAPTER NO. 8.   NERVOUS TISSUE

Nervous tissue is ectodermal in origin. Main properties of nervous tissue are irritability and conductivity. Hence its main function is transmission (conductivity) of impulse (irritability i.e. sensitivity of stimuli) to and from the central nervous system. Most of the nerve cells are present in the central nervous system (Brain & spinal cord). Processes of the nerve cells extend in central nervous system, while some of them reach the peripheral organs like muscles etc. these form the peripheral nervous system.

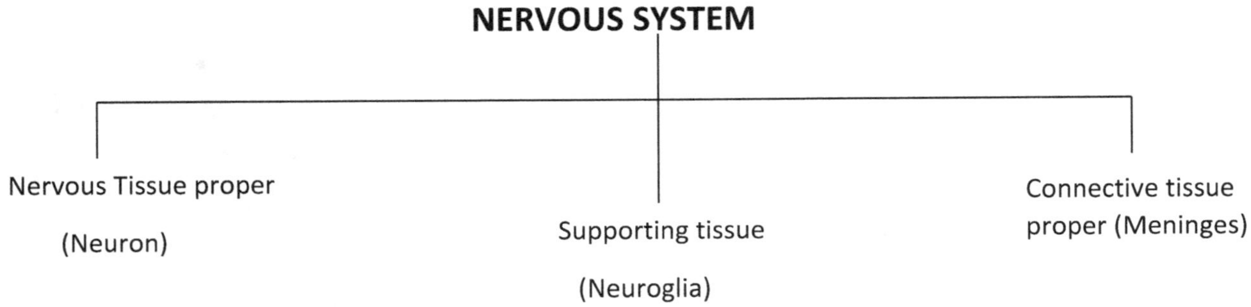


**Neuron-** Is the structural & functional unit of nervous system.

# NEURON

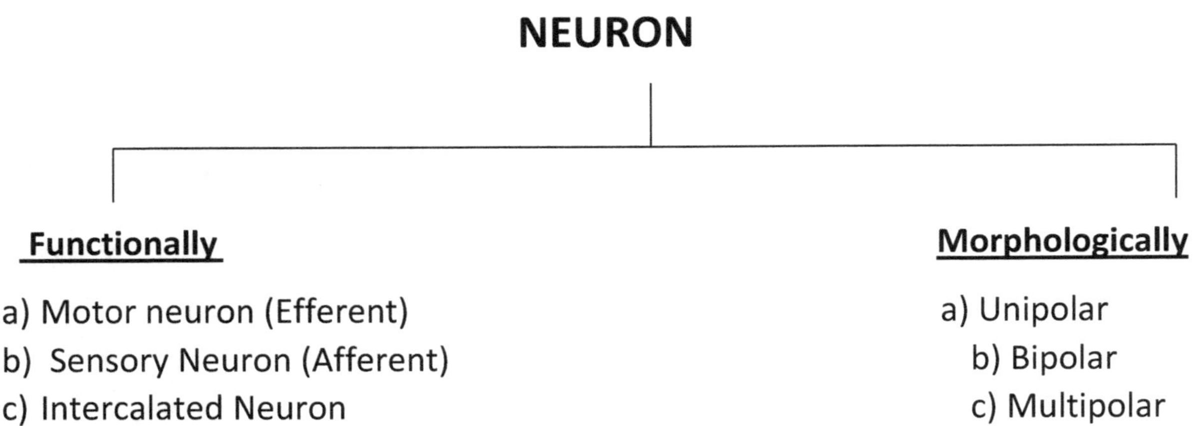


a) **Unipolar cells-**Present in spinal ganglion. They are actually pseudounipolar cells; globular in shape. They have one central and one peripheral process coming from a common stem.

b) **Bipolar cells-** present in retinal and olfactory mucosa. Cells are spindle shaped with central and peripheral processes coming from each end, of the cell.

c) **Multi polar cells-** commonest type present in CNS. Cells may be stellate, pyramidal or pear shaped. They have many processes coming from cell body; one long axon and other dendrites.

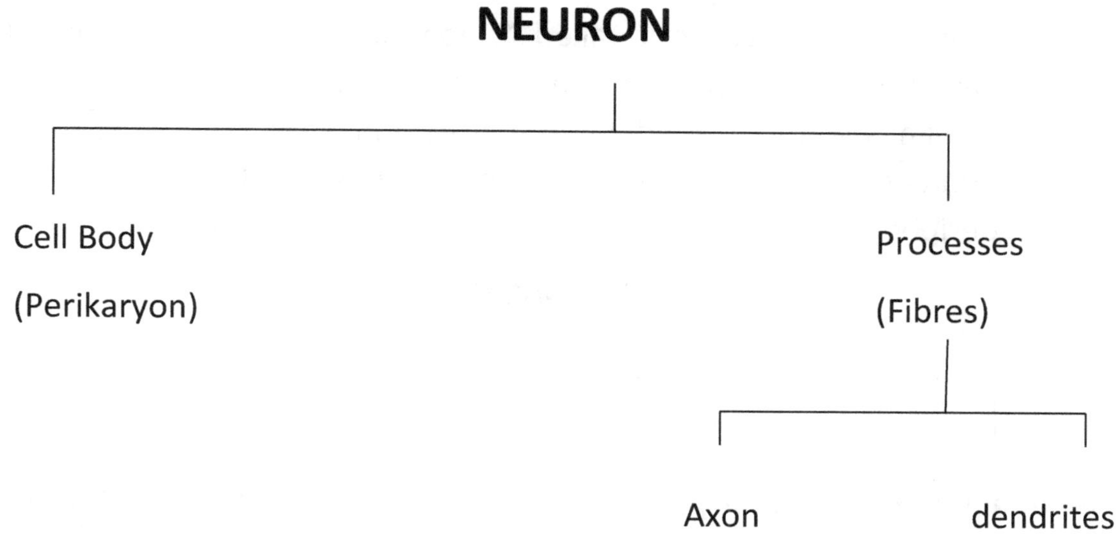


**Cell body-** the cell body and the processes have the outer covering of plasma membrane which is the site of impulses. The nerve cells are mostly large cells; may be unipolar, bipolar or multipolar. The nucleus is large and centrally placed. It is vesicular and nucleolus is very prominent. The nerve cells not multiply after birth.

Neuro-filaments are present in the cell body as well as the processes; but the exact function of these is not clear. Nissl granules are present in the cell body and dendrites but the absent in axon and base of axon called as axon hillock. Nissl granules stain with basic dyes as they are RER. The ribonucleo-proteins take the basic dye. Hence with H & E the Nissl granules appear as dark blue flakes in the cytoplasm. They are the site of synthesis of neuroplasm. The nerve cell in H & E the Nissl granules appear as dark blue flakes in the cytoplasm. They are site of synthesis of neuroplasm. The nerve cell in H & E section appears large cell; rounded or irregular with basophilic cytoplasm containing Nissl bodies (blue) and a large vesicular (open) nucleus with a prominent nucleolus.

**Cell Processes** – They are for conduction of impulses.

> Dendrites are receiver. The typical dendrite is broad at the base and tapers giving number of branches like a free. It ends very near the cell body. The dendrite contains Nissil bodies like the cell.

> Axon – It is a single process. It is uniform till its end where numbers of branches are given out called "Telodendria". Starts at axon hillock (conical elevation of the cell); it contains no Nissl substances. Its sheath called as myelin sheath, formed by the Schwann cells. These nerve fibres run in bundles. These bundles form the "Tracts" of C.N.S and "Nerves" in the peripheral N.S.

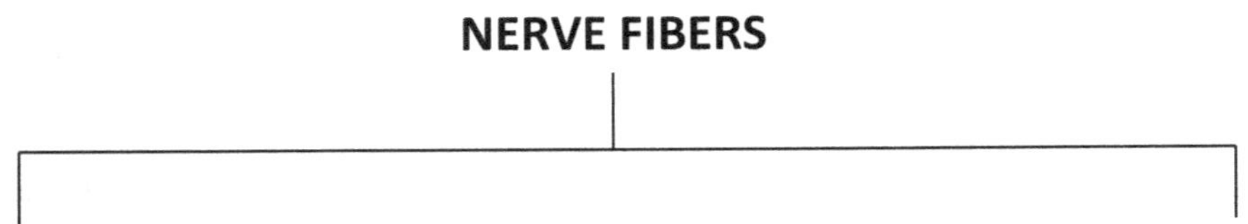


**Medullated or white or myelinated**

**Fibers**

a) Axis cylinder in the centre covered by Myelin sheath.
b) Medullary sheath; Shows constrictions called nodes of Ranvier.
c) Outer most layer or sheath know as neurilemmal sheath or Schwann sheath. This sheath helps in regeneration of nerve fibers. This sheath is absent in the fibers present in C.N.S.

**Nonmedullated of grey**

**Fibers**

a) No medullary sheath.

b) Only neurilemmal sheath

c) Present in post ganglionic fibers

Medullary sheath is formed by the Schwann cells. The plasma membrane of the cell winds round the axon during development. The internal distance represents one single Schwann cell. Collaterals come out at the nodes. The medullary sheath is mostly lipid in composition (Plasma membrane): hence it is dissolved during histological techniques.

Hence the medullary sheath is absent in H & E sections. The medullary sheath is stained with special stains like osmic acid.

**Grey and White Matter–**

Grey Matter- It has cell bodies of neurons; Fibres present are unmylinated. Neuroglia and blood vessels are also present .

White Matter- No cell bodies of neurons are there. Fibres present are mylinated hence white colour (myelin sheath). Neuroglia and blood vessels arrangement of grey matter and white matters differs in different parts of brain and spinal cord.

**Peripheral Nerves:**

They are collections of processes of neurons outside the CNS. The entire nerve is surrounded by a dense layer of connective tissue called Epineurium. The nerve consists of number of fascicule; each of which is surrounding by connective tissue called perineurium. Each fasciculus (bundle of fibres) consists of number of nerve fibres (axon). Each nerve fibre is surrounded by a layer of connective tissue called endoneurium.

## GANGLION

Ganglion – it is collection of cell bodies of neurons outside the brain & spinal cord.

| Sympathetic Ganglion | Spinal Ganglion |
|---|---|
| ➤ Found in sympathetic ganglion chain | ➤ Found in posterior root of a spinal nerve. |
| ➤ Ganglion covered by fibrous covering | ➤ Ganglion covered by fibrous covering |
| ➤ Cells are multipolar but of uniform size; Ganglion uniformly scattered through and are separated by nonmedullated nerve fibers. | ➤ Cells are unipolar of large size, some are of small size, arranged peripherally. Groups are separated by the medullated nerve fibers. |
| ➤ Every cell has cellular sheath (capsule). Nucleus is eccentrically placed & nucleolus is clearly seen as dark dot. | ➤ Every cell has cellular sheath (capsule). Nucleus is centrically placed & nucleolus is clearly seen as dark dot. |
| ➤ No space between the capsule and cell wall as the cell is multipolar. | ➤ There is always space between the capsule and cell wall as cell shrink during slide preparation. |

## NEUROGLIA

These cells form a kind of connective tissue for brain cells and spinal cord cells. Their function is to support. They are much smaller than neurons. In slide only nuclei are seen as dots. Processes required special staining e.g. silver impregnation.

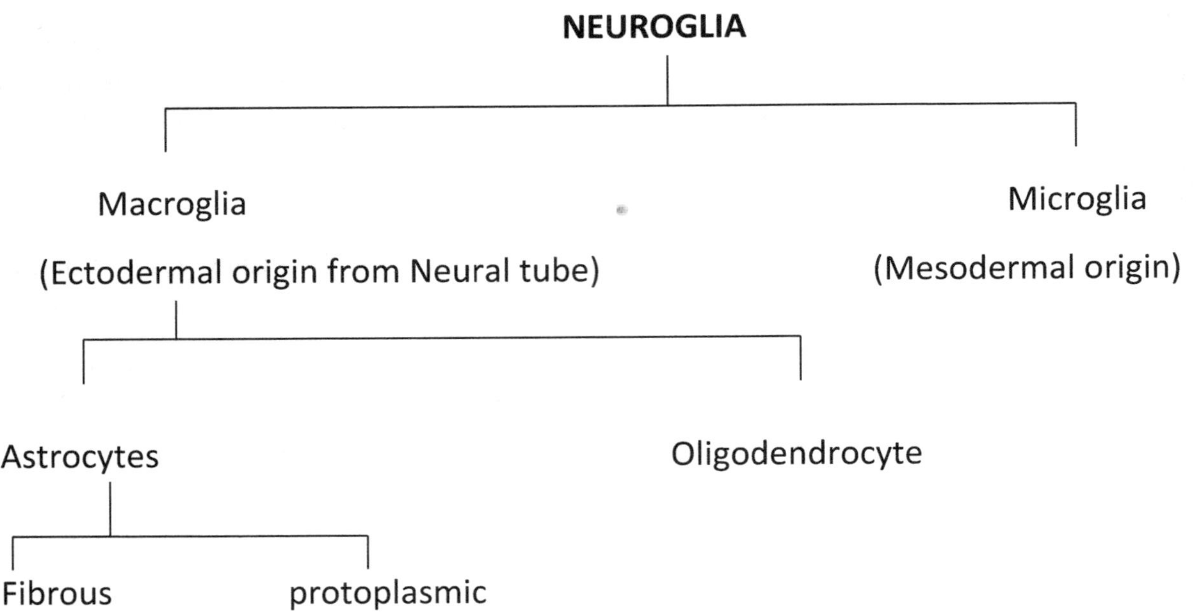


1) **Fibrous Astrocytes** - Cells with thick and symmetrical Processes present in the white matter, or CNS.
2) **Protpplasmic Astrocytes** -Cells with thick and symmetrical process. Present in the Grey matter. They surround the neurons of CNS.
3) **Oligodendrocyte** - Small round cells present in CNS. Functions like Schwann cells of PNS in myelination of nerve fibres. Processes are scanty.
4) **Microglia** - They are smallest flattened cells. Process short, found near capillaries.

**FUNCTION-** 1) Mechanical support. 2) Act as insulators. The nerve impulse is prevented from spreading in unwanted direction. 3) Oligodendrocytes provide myelin sheath to nerve in CNS.

**SYNAPSE –**It is the junction between two neurons. This point of contract may be (a) Axo-dendritic  (b) Axo- Axonal. A synapse transmits impulse from one neuron to other in only one direction. A neurotransmitter substance is released in the synaptic cleft. The substances are acetylcholine, adrenalin, noradrenalin etc. Physiologically a synapse may be excitatory or inhibitory.

**How to identify the slides:**

1) See the slide under low power first, and note ganglion?
2) Look for the size of cells uniform or two types?
3) Look for the space in between the capsule of the cells and the cell wall?
4) It is only from the general distribution of the cells in the ganglion that you can get the idea of what type of ganglion it is.
5) Cells of uniform size, uniformly scattered- Sympathetic ganglion.
6) Both large and small cells in groups- Spinal ganglion.

# PRACTICAL HINTS

1) **T.S. of modulated nerve (H & E)-** The nerve bundles cut across and  show many nerve fibres in them. Medullary sheath is dissolved, and you can see the central violet dot (axon) and a circular pink ring round around is (neurilemmal sheath) with a clear space in between the axon and the neurilemmal sheath. The clear space indicates medullary sheath. Each nerve fibre is surrounded by Epineurium.
2) **Teased nerve fibre (osmic acid stain)-**Fibres are stained black; Nodes of Ranvier are clearly seen. In these slides you will see the notched appearance of the medullary sheaths. But do not mix this with the clearly seen nodes of Ranvier.
3) **Nerve cells (Golgi stain)-**All the cells with their processes are stained jet black. Cellular details are not seen. Dendrites with their branching are clearly seen. You cannot make out the axons as they are cut across.
4) **Nerve cell (Nissle Stain)-**Slide stained with Thionine. See the nerve cell. Nucleus is clearly seen as a vacuole. Nucleolus is clearly seen as dark dot. Nissil bodies are seen as fine granules, scattered absent. Nissil granules are stained blue.

# NERVOUS TISSUE

## NERVE CELL (Neuron)

## Medullated nerve fibre (L.S.) (Osmic Acid Stain)

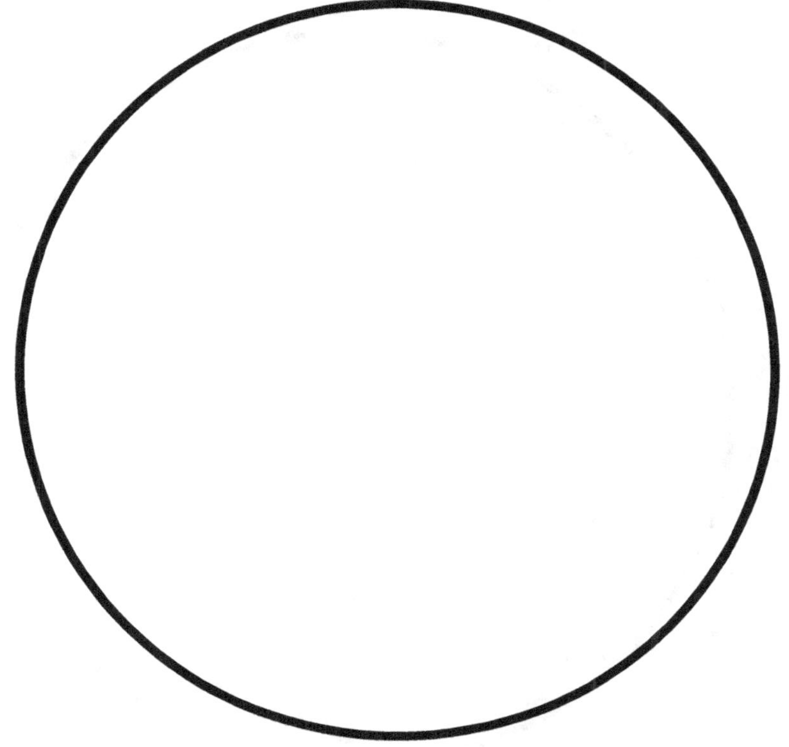

## MEDULLATED NERVE (T.S.) (H & E)

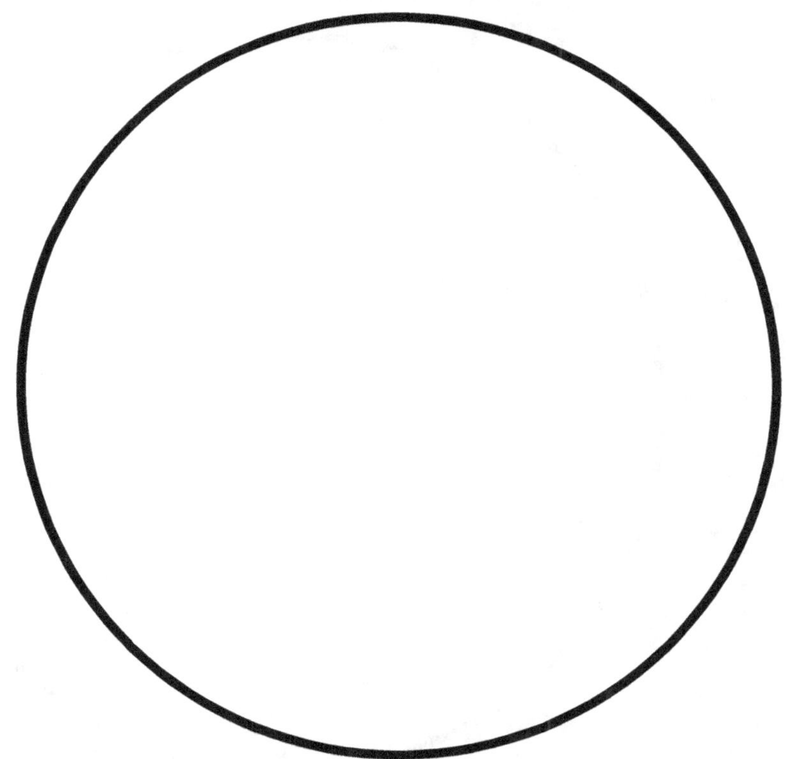

## Spinal Ganglion

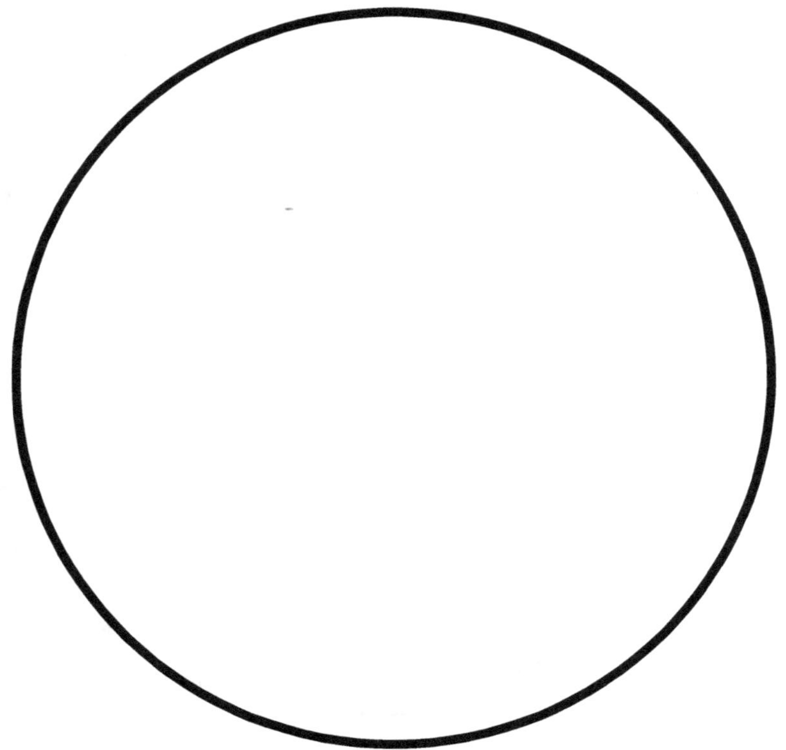

## Sympathetic Ganglion

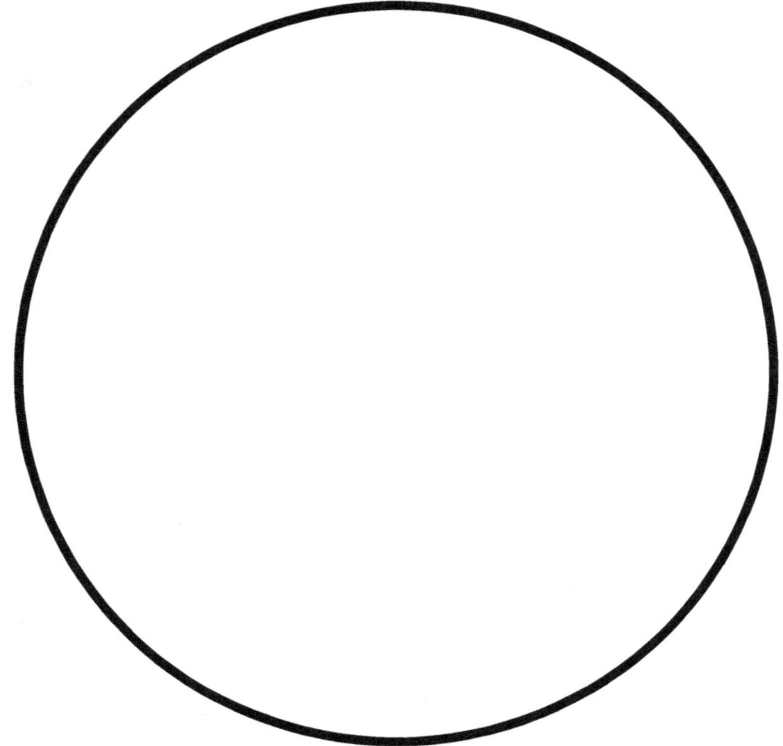

# CHAPTER NO.9. CIRCULATORY SYSTEM

The entire circulatory system is lined inside by endothelium. The vessels of the circulatory system are as fallows.

1) **Artery** - carry blood from heart to peripheral organs.
2) **Capillary** – simplest of vessel, present as capillary network in the tissue, organ system where actual exchange occurs.
3) **Veins-** return blood to heart.

## HISTOLOGICAL STRUCTURES

Blood vessels in general have three coats except the capillaries.

**Tunica Intima-** Innermost lining of single layer of squamous cells called as endothelium. Endothelial layer is supported by the subendothelial tissue made up of loose connective tissue which is separated from the tunica media by internal elastic lamina. Because of contraction of vessels the lamina appears collapsed.

**Tunica media-** Consists mainly of plain muscle fibres circularly arranged; interposed among the muscle fibres fenestrated elastic lamina of fibres. Smooth muscles cells are chief sites of metabolic activity of blood vessels. Type III collagen fibres are also present.

**Tunica Adventitia-** consists of connective tissue with some elastic fibres. This fuses with surrounding structures. Deeper there is external elastic lamina.

**<u>Capillary</u>** – structurally simplest vessel. It consists of single layer of endothelial cells of mesenchymal origin. The cells rest on basal lamina. Pericytes outside the basal lamina may be present.

## CAPILLARY

1) Continuous capillary     2) Fenestrated     3. Sinusoidal capillary

1) **Continuous capillary** – minute branches of arterioles form capillary bed; lined by single continuous layer of endothelium.

2) **Fenestrated or Perforated capillary-** the endothelial cells of fenestrated capillary show gaps where there is no cytoplasm but only the basement membrane form the diaphragm sealing the gaps at the same time allowing rapid exchange e.g. present in the kidney and endocrines for rapid exchange.

3) **Sinusoidal capillary-**

   1) Absence of continuous lining of endothelial cell
   2) Very wide in diameter with very slow circulation.
   3) Phagocytic cells present in the walls.
   4) Absence of continuous basal lamina.

Present in liver, bone, spleen where interchange of cells, is enhanced by gaps.

## <u>Artery</u>- varies in size and contents of wall according to the functional need.

1. <u>**Elastic Artery**</u> – These are the Large Arteries and also called as Conducting Artery as they carry the blood from heart to the muscular arteries. Aorta Pulmonary trunk and their branches are the examples of elastic artery.

   - **Tunica intima** consists of endothelium made up of simple squamous epithelium resting on basal lamina, subendothelial connective tissue which is loose connective tissue consisting of elastic fibres. Internal elastic lamina of elastic fibres is present but difficult to distinguish from the elastic lamina of tunica media.

   - **Tunica media** – it is thickest layer, consisting of high amount of elastic fibres in the form of elastic lamellae. In human Aorta, about 50 elastic lamellae are present. Some smooth muscles and collagen type III fibres are present in between the elastic lamellae.

   - **Tunica adventitia** – is formed by loose connective tissue, consisting of elastic fibres, collagen fibres, fibroblasts, macrophages, mast cells, blood vessels (vasa vasorum). It also consists of nerve bundles and lymphatic vessels.

2. **Muscular Artery -** These are medium sized arteries having diameter of lumen 2-10 mm. It is also called as distributing artery as it send blood to different parts of the body.

   - **Tunica intima** -  It consists of endothelium (which is simple squamous epithelium) resting on the basement membrane. Subendothelial connective tissue is minimal or absent. Internal elastic lamina is distinctly visible and seen in wavy appearance.

- **Tunica Media** – It is made up of circularly arranged smooth muscles. More than 2/3 of wall of artery is made from tunica media. Type III collagen fibres and few elastic fibres are also present.
- **Tunica Adventitia** – It is made up of connective tissue with different fibres and cells.

3. **End arteries-** are those arteries which have no precapillary anastomosis. Vasa recti of intestines, splenic arteries, central artery of retina etc. are examples.

4. **Vasa Vasorum-** are those arteries which supply the walls of big arteries. These are the branches either of that artery or of other vessels which are in the neighbourhood. They supply the adventitia and outer two third of the media. The inner media gets nourishment by diffusion from the blood in the vessels itself.

5. **Helicine Arteries-** are the arteries which open directly into a cavernous space (penis) and not in capillary bed. Its media is of circular muscle fibres and very thick.

## VEINS

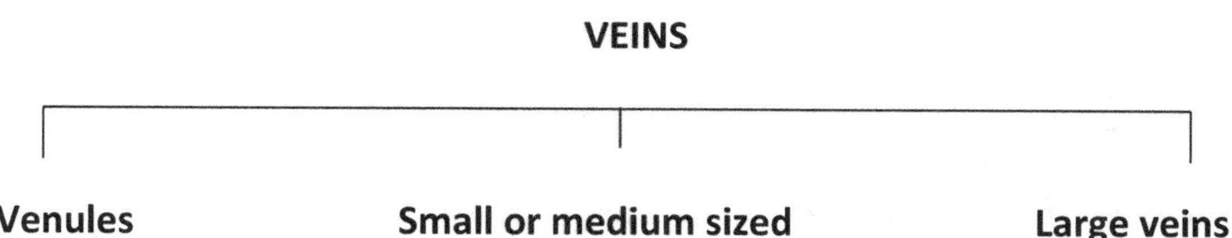



**Veins-** also have 3 layers, Tunica Intima, Tunica Media and Tunica Adventitia, but Tunica Media is much smaller than Tunica adventitia. These three layers can be identified in large veins but difficult to differentiate in medium and small sized veins.

Tunica Intima – Endothelial cells resting on basement membrane are seen. Sub-endothelial connective tissue is less in amount. Internal elastic lamina is absent.

Tunica Media- This layer is thinner than tunica media of same sized artery. It consists of smooth muscles, collagen fibres, fibroblasts.

Tunica adventitia – This is thickest layer of vein. It is loose connective tissue and consists of smooth muscle cells, collagen fibres, elastic fibres, fibroblasts. In large veins, the smooth muscle cells and elastic fibres are longitudinally oriented to sustain stretching of vein.

**Exceptions-** veins of pregnant uterus have thick muscle coat in their media. So also umbilical veins and veins of limbs (lower specially); veins of the brain and spinal cord, bone marrow and retina have no muscular coat.

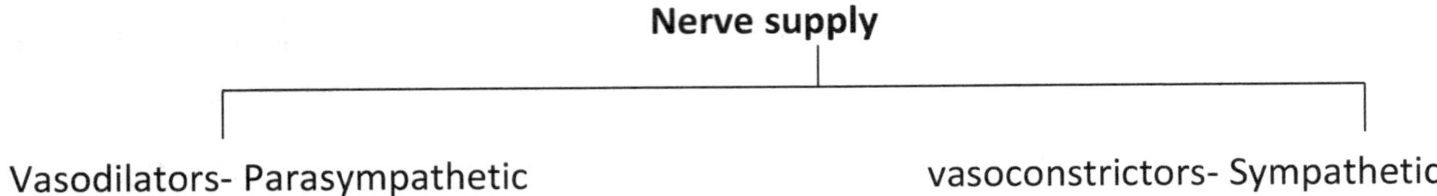


## PRACTICAL HINTS

1) Slide of artery and vein together (H & E stain). Move the field and see differences in both. Note the wall of both the vessels. See the differences in the wall of both the vessels. Artery is thick walled with rounded lumen.  Vein is thin walled and appears collapsed.
2) Large sized artery T.S. of aorta. Concentrate and focus at Tunica Media. See the large number of the elastic fibres.
3) Slide of liver for sinusoids and Kupffer's cells.

### QUESTION:
1) What are sinusoids? How do they differ from the capillaries?
2) Name the organs where you find the sinusoids?
3) How does the T. Media and T.Intima receive their blood supply?
4) What is the main microscopic appearance of the arterioles?
5) Are there any muscle fibres in blood vessel? If so in what type of blood vessels do you get it? What type of muscle fibres you get in those vessels?
6) What vessels possess elastic laminae?
7) Why the arteries do not collapse when empty?
8) Why the intimal layers look corrugated fixed preparation of artery?
9) What is the function of elastic tissue in T. Adventitia?

10) What is the function of collagen fibres in T. Adventitia?

11) What parts of the blood vessels do the vasa-vasorum supply?

## LARGE SIZE ARTERY (ELASTIC)

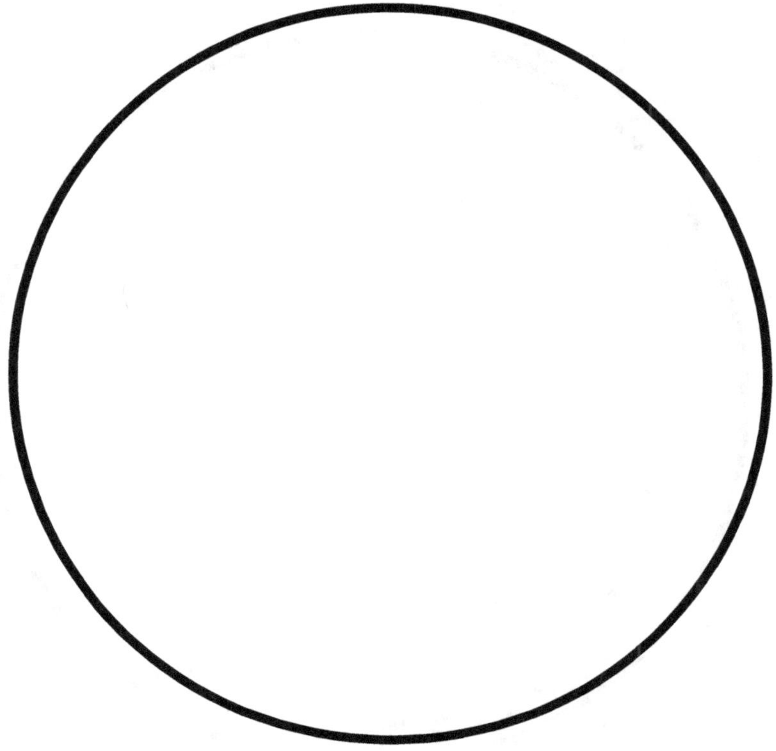

## MEDIUM SIZE ARTERY (MUSCULAR)

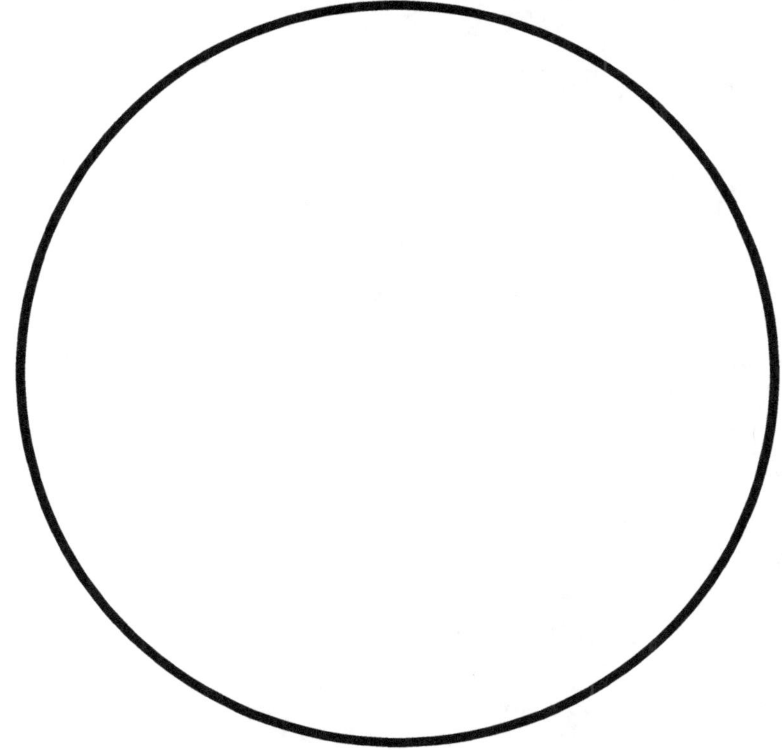

# Vein

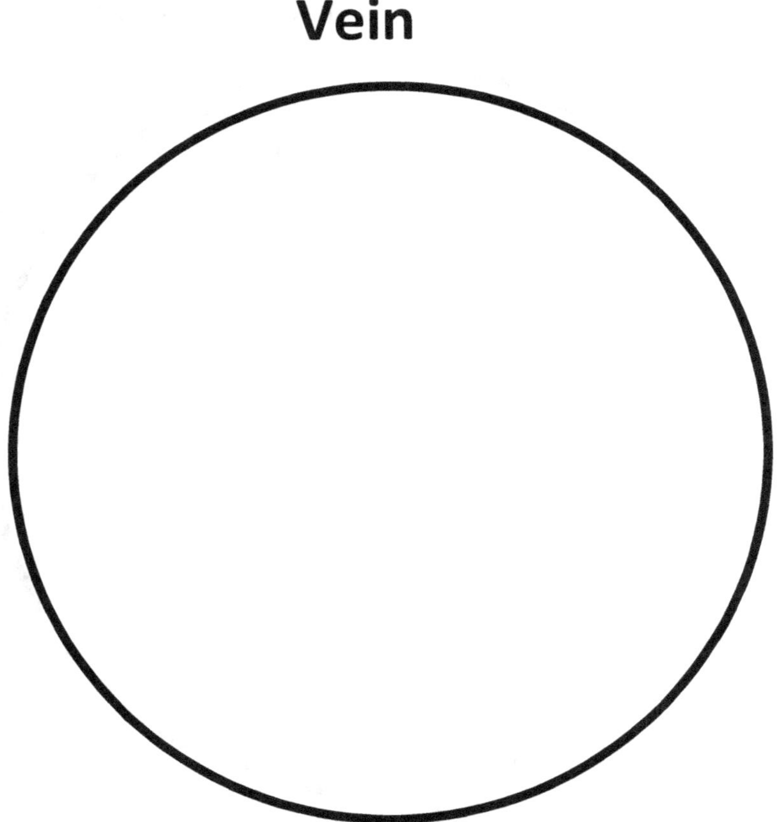

# CHAPTER NO. 10  LYMPHOID TISSUE

## 1. <u>LYMPH NODE</u>

These are bean shaped bodies scattered throughout the body. They are present in axilla, groin, along blood vessels in the neck, thorax, abdomen and pelvis.

**Structure in General:**

1) It has a hilum through which the afferent lymph vessels enter in. Afferent lymph vessels at the periphery carrying from areas of drainage to the glands for filtration.
2) It has a capsule which sends trabeculae into the substance of the gland. Trabeculae divide the lymph node into number of compartments.
3) It has a reticular network of reticular fibres, present throughout the gland. The network gives support to the free lymphocytes present here.
4) Section of lymph node shows two zones, outer dense zone 'cortex' and inner loosely arranged zone the 'medulla'.
5) Lymph follicles- are situated at the periphery, just under the capsules in the cortex. Some of them show germinal centres.
6) Para cortical zone between cortex and medulla contains 'T' Lymphocytes. Cells are densely packed. 'T' cells are thymus dependent cells. If thymus is removed these cells disappear. They give rise to cell mediated antigen response e.g. graft rejection. The rest of the lymphocytes of lymph nodes are 'B' lymphocytes.
7) Medulla consists of loosely arranged large number of sinusoids and lymphocytes and macrophages. The lymph filters through gland, coming from afferent vessels at the periphery, going through sinusoids. Thus, macrophage cells remove the foreign particles. Lymph is returned by efferent vessel from hilum.

## Slide of lymph node (H & E stain).

Have a general look of the section under low power. Identify the cortex and the medulla. See the capsule and the trabeculae. Identify the lymph follicles (nodules), which are peripherally arranged in cortex of the gland.

**Identification of the slide**- lymphoid tissue with the follicles arranged at the periphery (IMP) sub capsular lymph follicles; some showing germinal centres ( a lightly stained area in the centre of the follicle). Trabeculae are seen, capsule is visible.

**QUESTION :**

1) What is a lymphoid follicle? When does it appear?
2) What is germinal centre?
3) How is lymph filtered in the lymph node?

## 2. THYMUS

Thymus is bilobed structure present in the superior mediastium. It is well developed from birth to puberty. After puberty it becomes smaller in size, the process is called involution of the gland.

1) **Structure in general**- glands are enclosed in a connective tissue capsule, made up of collagen fibres, which send in the substance of the gland dividing it into many incomplete lobules.
2) Each lobule consists of outer dense zone (cortex) and a central zone of loosely packed cells ( medulla).
3) Cortex consists of densely packed lymphocytes.
4) Medulla consists of loosely packed lymphocytes with Hassall's corpuscles in it.
5) Thymic or Hassall's corpuscles. These are degenerated epitheloid cells concentrically arranged. These is very typical of thymus gland (IMP)
   Hassall's corpuscles stain dark pink in H & E. they appear pink laminated structure.

**Epithellal cells**- They are derived from endoderm of the pharynx. They are flattened cells with number of branches producing a kind of cellular reticulam in thymus under the capsule, along the trabeculae and blood vessels. They form the blood thymus barrier.

**Function of thymus-** The lymphocytes of the thymus comes from bone marrow and multiplies in thymus. Production of "T - lymphocytes" is the main function. These cells can recognise foreign protein and attack them. They are produced here and released in the blood. They are also settled in other lymphoid organs like lymph nodes, spleen etc. where they produce more 'T' lymphocytes.

**Identification of the slide- (H & E stain)**
Capsule and the trabeculae are seen. Identify the pink stained concentrically arranged Hassall's corpuscle (imp).
Lobules incompletely formed. Each lobule shows cortex medulla appearance.

**QUESTION:**
1) What is the main identification point of the slide of thymus gland?
2) What are Hassel's or thymic corpuscle?
3) What are the age changes in thymus gland?

3. **TONSILS**

**Epithelium-** surface of the tonsils and their crypts are lined by stratified squamous epithelium moist variety of the oval cavity.
**Lymph Nodules-** are seen beneath the epithelium and have a germinal centre. These nodules are arranged around tonsilar crypts.

1) **Slide of tonsil (H & E stain)-**look for the lymphoid tissue in general.
2) See the tonsilar crypts lined by stratified squamous epithelium.
3) See the lymph nodules arranged parallel round the tonsilar crypts.

**Main point-** for identification- the tonsilar crypts are lined by stratified squamous epithelium and large amount of lymphoid tissue round about them. Lymph nodules are arranged parallel to the crypts.

## 4. SPLEEN

1) **Structural plan-** Capsules made up of collagen, elastic and plain muscle, fibres.
2) Trabeculae divide the substance of the spleen into zones of lymphoid tissue (splenic pulp).

   Thin reticular fibres form a network in the substance of the spleen to support the loose cells.

### SPLENIC PULP

| White pulp | Red Pulp |
|---|---|
| Consist of densely packed lymphocytic Collection. (malpighian corpuscle) that surrounds arterioles. Malpighian corpuscle has a germinal centre. The amount of white pulp lessens as the age advances. | Is an area of loosely packed cells, occupying the space in between the sinuses and the Malpighian corpuscles. This consists of RBCs and Lymphocytes are both of 'T' & 'B' Types. |

**White Pulp:** The lymphocytes of the Malpighian corpuscle of the white pulp consist of 'B' lymphocytes in the germinal centre area while elsewhere consist of 'T' lymphocytes. The arteriole may be eccentrically placed. More than one blood vessel may be seen in white pulp.

**Splenic circulation-** Splenic artery branches out in the substance of the spleen, branches go through the trabeculae. Arterioles are surrounded by lymphocytes. Arterioles sub branch into 5 to 6 smaller straight branches (penicillin).

**Pencilli-** branch out to form very fine shelter capillaries. Capillaries open into the venous sinusoids which open into trabecular vein and from there in to the splenic vein.

    **i) Splenic circulation-** capillaries open into the splenic pulp directly and then the blood cells get into substance of the spleen forming red pulp. The blood enters into the venous sinuses by diffusion.(open circulation).

ii) The capillaries open into the venous sinuses directly, and communicate with them, (closed circulation). However blood elements are allowed to enter the substances to form red pulp by the blood vessels.

## PRACTICAL HINTS.

Identification of the slide of spleen ( H& E Stain).

1) See the lymphoid tissue in general.
2) Look for the Malpighian corpuscles as lymphoid tissue collection and its central blood vessels ( arterioles).
3) Malpighian corpuscle are scattered throughout the field.
4) See the red pulp.
5) Trabeculae and the capsule can be seen. Scattered Malpighian corpuscles with their central blood vessels. (arteriole) and the red pulp are the identifying points.

### NOTE ON LYMPHOCYTE

Lymphocytes may be small or large. They are also called 'B' lymphocyte (Bursa dependent lymphocyte). In birds the 'B' lymphocytes are produced in the Bursa of fabricius. Hence the name Bursa dependent lymphocytes. In human being Bursa of Fabricus is not present and the 'B' lymphocytes are produced in the bone marrow.

The 'T' lymphocytes are produced in the thymus and circulate and get settled in other organs like lymph node, spleen. The 'B' lymphocytes are also present. In thymus only 'T' lymphocytes are present. The 'T' lymph node can recognise foreign proteins and destroy by cell mediated response. While the 'B' lymphocytes when comes in contact with the foreign proteins (antigens) turns to become a plasma cell and forms antibodies. The antigen antibody reaction occurs. Lymphocyte in general forms the defence mechanism of the body, to fight the foreign in the form of bacteria etc.

**LYMPH NODE**

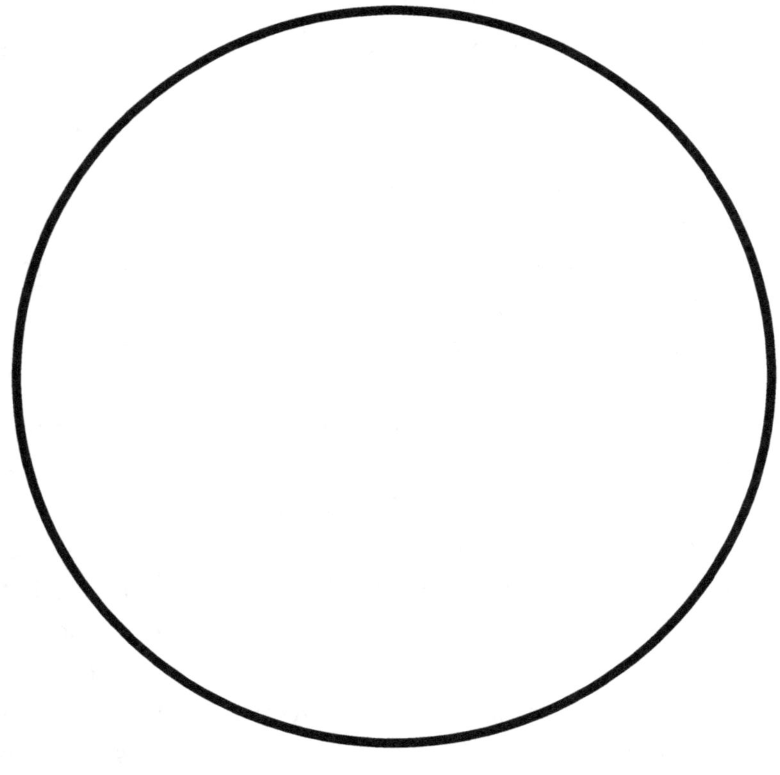

**SPLEEN**

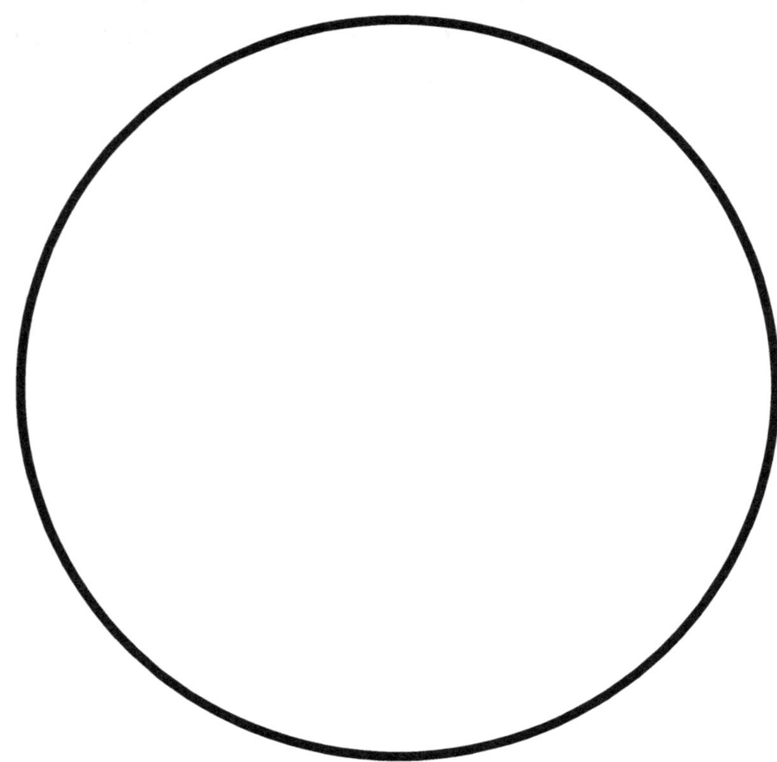

## TONSIL

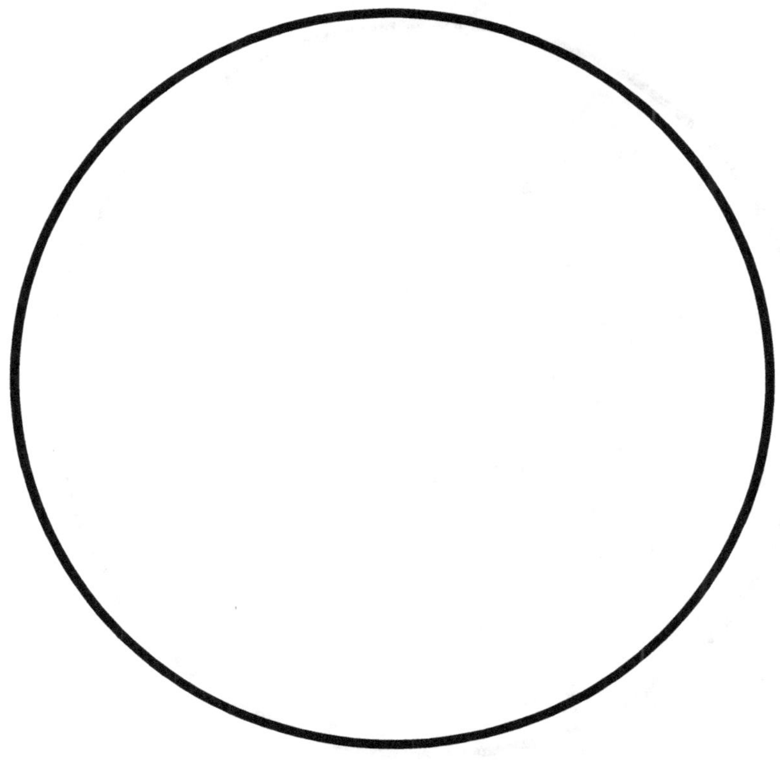

## THYMUS

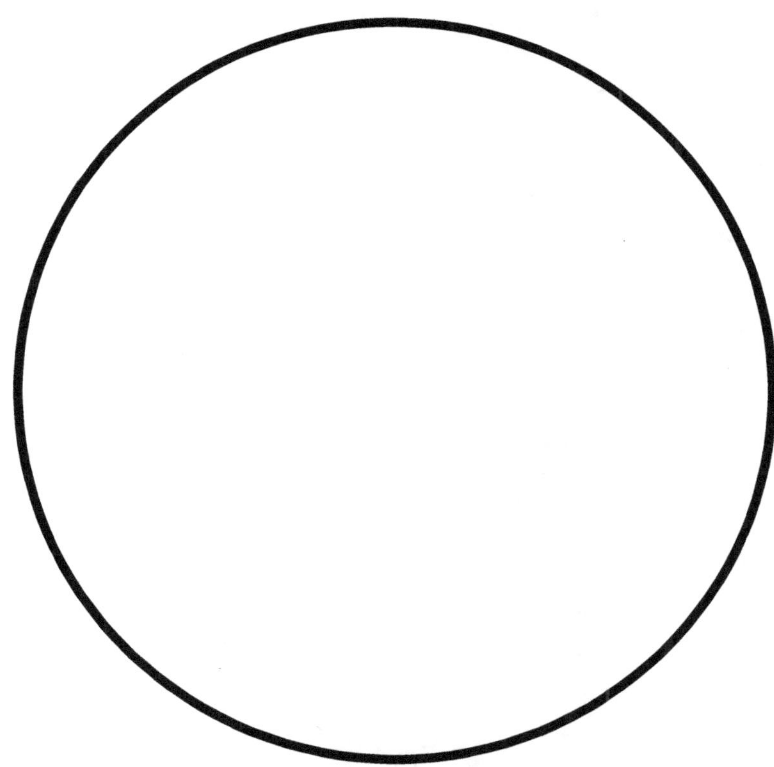

## PEYERS PATCH (Ileum)

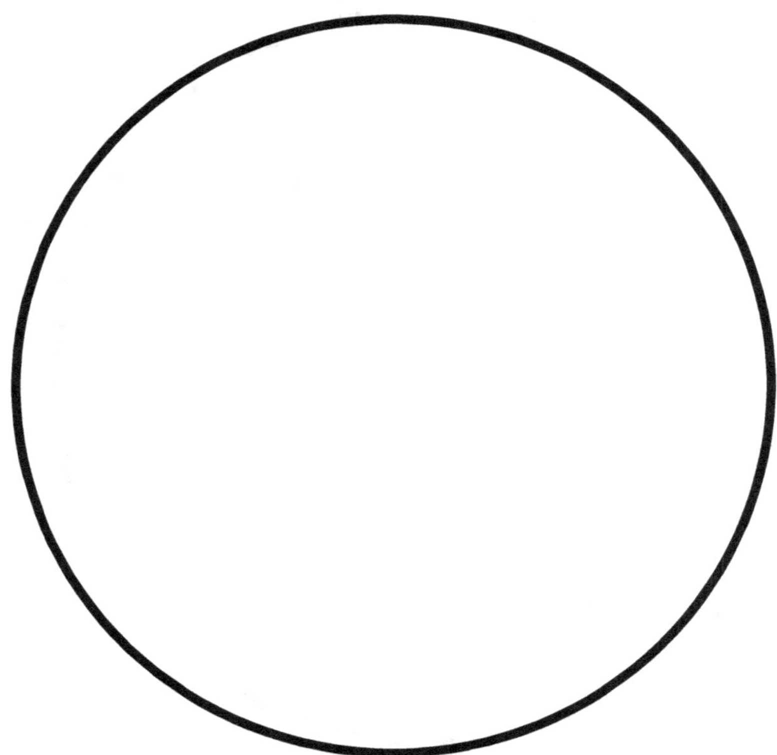

# CHAPTER NO. 11  RESPIRATORY SYSTEM

This system consists of two portions having different functions.

1) **Conducting passages-** starts with nasal cavity, pharynx, larynx, trachea; bronchi branching repeatedly to smaller bronchi & bronchioles connecting to the proper respiratory tissue i.e. alveoli of lung and thus carrying air to and from the lungs.
2) **Respiratory part-** this is the place where the gases are exchanged i.e. the respiratory bronchioles, alveolar ducts, alveoli or air sacs of the lungs.

**General description of conducting passages-**
1) **Wall** – consists of either bone, cartilage to keep the passage patent. Connective tissue binding these hard parts together and some smooth muscle is present. The cartilages are bigger in upper respiratory passage but as bronchi branch and re-branch they become smaller and in respiratory bronchioles the cartilages are absent. The smooth muscle controls the lumen of bronchi. Sympathetic nerves are bronchodilator (relax smooth muscle). While vagus, the parasympathetic nerve contracts the smooth muscle of the bronchioles.
2) **Epithelium-** is pseudo stratified ciliated columnar with plenty of goblet cells. Epithelium is kept moist by serous glands and mucous glands present in lamina propria. The cilia help to remove dust etc.
Blood vessels are plenty in the sub-mucosa to warm the air conducted through the passages before it reaches the lungs.

### 1. EPIGLOTTIS

It is elastic leaf like structure situated at the opening of larynx. It guards the laryngeal opening during swallowing. So that, no food particles enter the larynx.
**Histology-** centrally placed elastic cartilage, stratified squamous epithelium (moist type) is covering on both sides of epiglottis except lower posterior part which is lined by pseudostratified ciliated columnar epithelium. Sero-mucous glands are situated underneath the epithelium in the lamina propria consisting of connective fibres.

## 2. TRACHEA

The tracheal tube is kept patent by 15 to 20 hyaline cartilages which are 'C' shaped. The cartilages are bound together by fibrous connective tissue. Posteriorly the two ends of 'C' are connected by tracheal muscles to form a tube. The tube is lined inside by mucous membrane.

1) **Mucous membrane-** Pseudo stratified ciliated columnar epithelium with large numbers of goblet cells are seen.
2) **Submucosa-** is made up of loose areolar tissue and contains sero-mucous glands.
3) **Cartilage-** Horseshoe shaped hyaline cartilage is surrounded by perichondrium. The gap behind the two ends of cartilage is filled by smooth muscle fibres (trachealis muscle). Functions of trachealis muscle is to allow free passage of food through oesophagus. It allows dilation of the oesophagus when the food bolus is passing through it. The oesophagus is the immediate posterior relation to trachea.

**Identification of the slide of Trachea-** tube like structure, showing-
1) Pseudostratified ciliated columnar epithelium.
2) "C" shaped cartilage ring in one piece (may be more than one).
3) Goblet cells and seromucous glands seen in submuscosa.
4) The gap on the posterior aspect of 'C' shaped cartilage rings is filled by trachealis muscle (smooth muscle).

## 3. BRONCHUS

Bronchus is smaller in diameter than trachea. Structure is same as seen in trachea, but the cartilage is always in smaller pieces usually more than two in number; smooth muscle fibres are seen in lamina propria deep to epithelium. The smooth muscles are under autonomic control. Presence of smooth muscle in lamina propria under the epithelium is very characteristic of bronchi.

## 4. TERMINAL BRONCHIOLES

It is distal part of conducting passage. It has diameter of about 1 mm and prominent mucosal folds.

<u>Epithelium</u>- simple columnar epithelium; few goblet cells.

Plain muscle fibres forming ring round the bronchioles, cartilage and glands are absent.

## 5. RESPIRATORY BRONCHIOLES
- Lining epithelium is cuboidal type.
- No glands; no cilia; no goblet cells.
- Thick ring of plain muscle fibres prominently seen.

## 6. LUNG ALVEOLI
These are air sacs, having thin walls lined by simple squamous epithelium (imp). These are surrounded by large number of blood vessels and reticular fibres. There are two types of alveolar CELLS.

- **Pneumocyte I**- These are squamous cells lining the alveolar walls. They are respiratory in functions
- **Pneumocyte II**- They are round secretary cells. Secrete a substance called pulmonary surfactant. This surfactant makes a thin film over the respiratory tube and reduce surface tension thus preventing collapse of alveolus during expirations.

## 7. ALVEOLAR SEPTA
Lung alveoli are cut in various planes hence it is difficult to find a complete alveolus. It shows this network of polygonal space, lined by simple squamous epithelium. Adjacent alveoli have common wall. Within this wall are capillary plexuses, supported by minimal connective tissue, which mostly in the form of reticular fibres.

A number of macrophages lymphocytes are present as defence cells. You may see bronchus, bronchiole if the section passes through one of them in the slides of the lung.

# IDENTIFICATION OF SLIDES:

1) **Nasal septum-** a central core of hyaline cartilage covered on both sides by pseudo stratified cilliated columnar epithelium. Lamina propria contains seromucous glands, olfactory nerves, lymphoid tissue etc.
2) **EPIGLOTTIS:** centrally placed elastic cartilage, stratified squamous epithelium (moist type) is covering on both sides of epiglottis, mucous glands are situated

underneath the epithelium in the lamina propria consisting of connective tissue fibres.

3) **Trachea-** a tubular organ. 'C' shaped hyaline cartilage ring present. The mucosa shows pseudo stratified ciliated columnar epithelium with plenty of goblet cells. posteriorly trachealis muscle fills the gap in the cartilage.

4) **Bronchus-** smaller in size than trachea. Hyaline cartilage present in the places where the wall is connected by connective tissue. The lumen is lined by mucous membrane with pseudo stratified columnar ciliated epithelium with number of goblet cells. Underneath the epithelium in the lamina propria, plain muscle fibres are present. This is the identifying feature of bronchus from trachea. In tracheas sub epithelial plain muscle fibres are present.

5) **Lung-** Spongy tissue. The alveoli are lined by flattened squamous cells. At places bronchi, bronchioles etc. are seen in the same section. Occasionally lymphoid follicles are present here and there. Respiratory bronchioles with wall of smooth muscle and no cartilage are prominent feature of lung.

**QUESTION:**

1)   Why do you say that it is a slide of trachea and not of bronchus?
2)   What are the other tubular organs in our body where we get ciliated epithelium?

**EPIGLOTTIS**

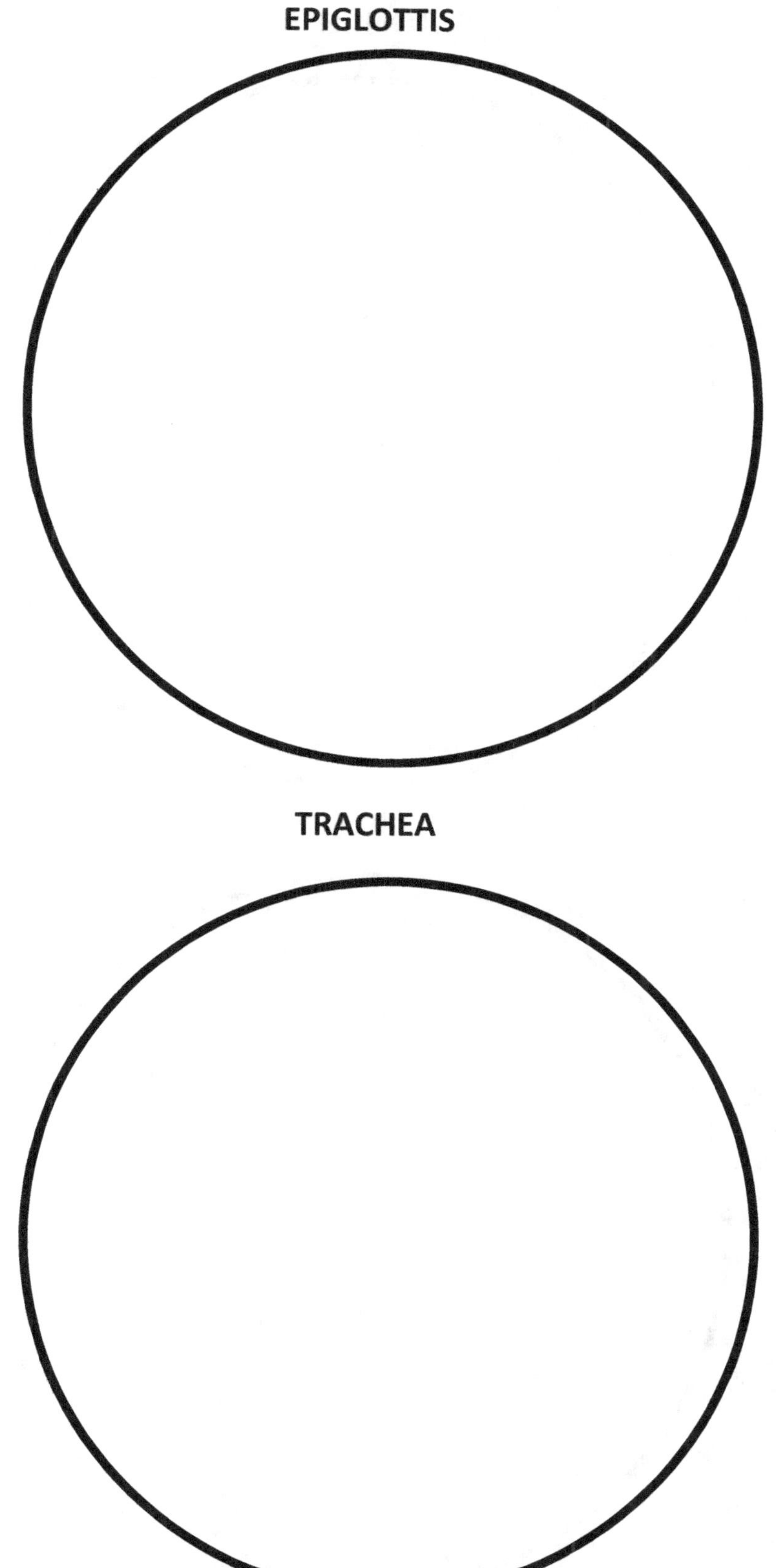

**TRACHEA

## BRONCHUS

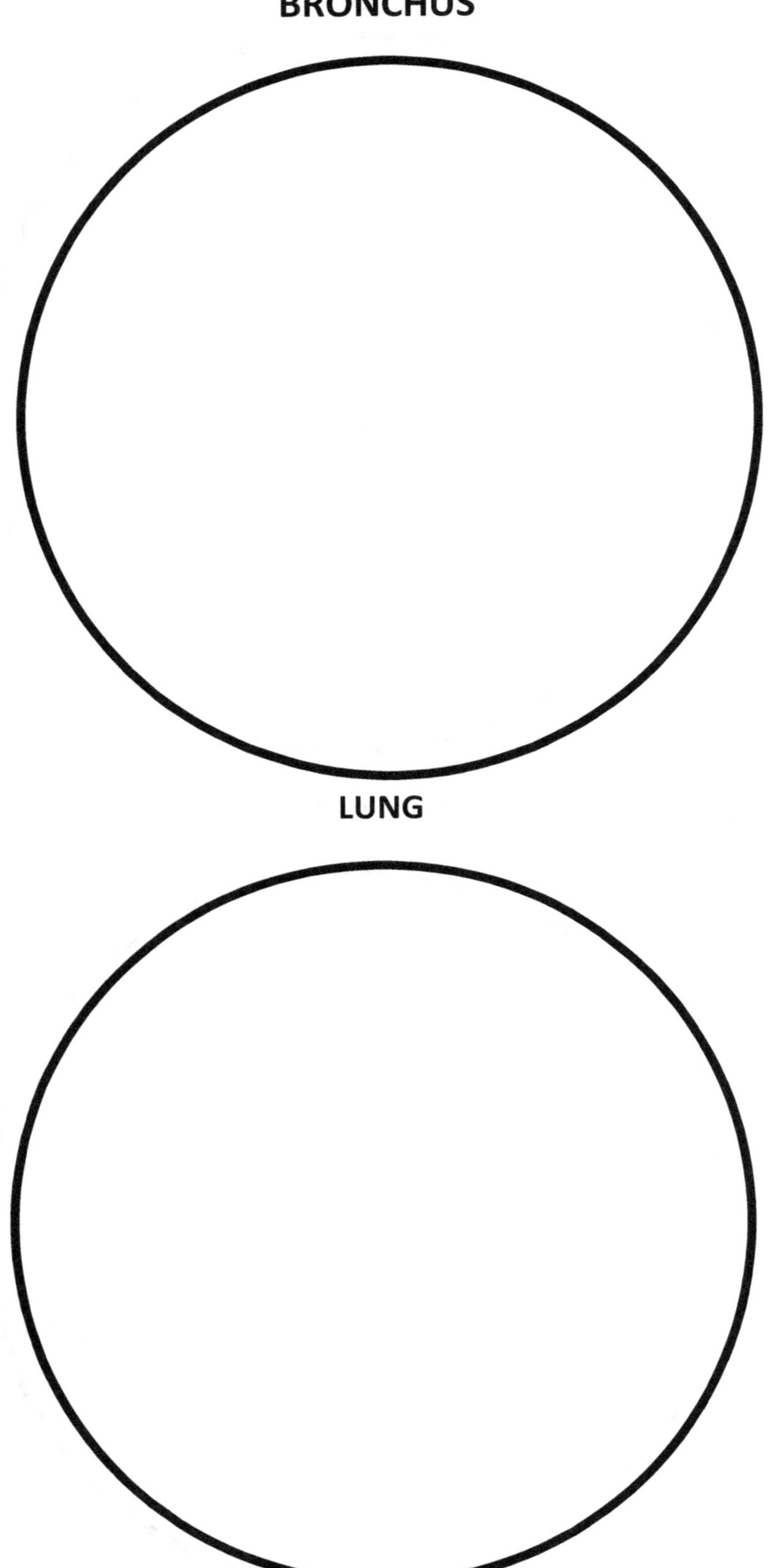

## LUNG

# CHAPTER NO 12.  DIGESTIVE SYSTEM

This consists of tube like structure, beginning from lips and ending at anus. Accessory structures associated with the digestive system are salivary glands, teeth, lip, tongue, liver and pancreas. The tube is composed of pharynx, oesophagus, stomach, small and large intestine and anal canal.

## 1. <u>DEVELOPING TOOTH</u>

**Enamel-** develops from ectoderm.

**Pulp, Dentin, Cementum-** develops from mesoderm.

I)   **Development stages-** Ridge is formed by endodermal thickening on the alveolar arch. (This is dental lamina).
II)   This lamina gives rise to dental buds.
III)  Penetration, thickening & proliferation of dental bud in to the underlying mesoderm continue. Each bud representing single tooth.
IV)  This enlargement of dental bud gets detached from surface epithelium and forms the enamel organ, which is like inverted cup, in the mesoderm underneath.
V)   Enamel organ is navigated from the deep surface, by the mesoderm forming a papilla, the dental papilla.
VI)  Enamel cells differentiate.

a)   **Ameloblast cells-** the cells in contact with the dental papilla. They are tall columnar cells. They lay down and as enamel is laid down these cells move towards the surface.
b)   **Enamel epithelium-** outermost layer of the cells, which are flat cells.
c)   **Stellate reticulum cells-** lie in between ameloblast cells and surface enamel epithelium. It is a network of stellate cells, with branching processes.

**Formation of dentine –**
a)   Odontoblast are formed by mesoderm cells of the papilla just deep to ameloblast cells. Both ameloblasts and odontoblast cells are in opposition. Odontoblasts are tall columnar cells with apical process. As dentine is formed by odontoblast, these cells move towards pulp cavity centrally leaving the apical processes of the cells in the dentinal tubules. The dentinal apical processes, which

form future dentinal fibres round which the dentinal canals are formed in the dentine giving a striated appearance of dentine. Predentin is formed by odontoblasts cells which get calcified later on.

In the central part of the mesodermal papilla the cells do not undergo any change, and forms the dental pulp; in which blood vessels develop and nerve enters.

## 2. TONGUE

Tongue is muscular organ covered by mucous membrane. The mucous membrane of dorsal side show papillae the elevations. On the ventral side mucous membrane is smooth.

### PAPILLAE

A papilla has epithelial covering with connective tissue core containing blood, vessels, nerves and Lymphatic's.

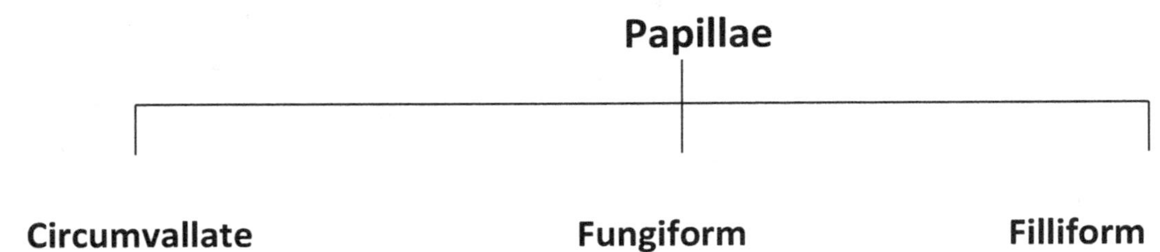


Tongue has a central core of voluntary muscles, which are cut in section. The mass of muscles is covered by mucous membrane which is rough elevated ( papillae) on the dorsum of the tongue and smooth on the ventral aspect.

**Epithelium**- Stratified squamous epithelium (moist type).

**Lamina propria** – contains sub mucus connective tissue, and serous, mucous glands.

**Muscle**- voluntary muscle fibres arranged transversely & show striations longitudinally.

**Taste buds**- special sensory organ of taste.  Barrel shaped structure embedded in the stratified squamous epithelium of the side wall of circumvallate papilla.

**Structure of taste bud-** Broad base touching the lamina propria. Open on the surface by minute hole (gustatory pore).  Consists of two types of cells.

a) **Gustatory cell-** slender columnar cell tapering at both ends. Has a distal hair like process (gustatory hair), which comes in contact with food material; and proximal long process. (the sensory fibre). The sensory fibre carries sense of taste; to the nerve.

b) **Sustentacular cells or supporting cell-** columnar cells. Broad at the base and narrow at the end. These cells support the gustatory cells.

**Identification of the slide of tongue:**
**Epithelium-** Stratified squamous epithelium (moist variety) large voluntary muscle bundles cut at various sections. Circumvallate papilla clearly seen with taste buds.


3. <u>**SALIVARY GLANDS**</u>

These are parotid, submandidular, and sublingual glands. All these are compound tubulo alveolar glands. Every gland has a capsule which sends in trabeculae and divides the gland into lobes and lobules. Branches of main duct are present in the trabeculae. They are called interlobar ducts. Smaller ducts enter the lobes (interlobular).

**Ducts-** Main ducts are lined by columnar epithelium.
**Small ducts-** lined by short columnar epithelium (cells showing basal striations).
**Large ducts-** lined by stratified columnar epithelium.
**Alveoli-** lined by pyramidal cells secreting either serous or mucous secretion. In between these cells are the branched cells, known as myoepithelial cells which are contractile. They help to squeeze out secretions from alveoli into ducts.

**Demilunes of heidenhain (Crescents of Gianuzzi) -** mucous alveoli are capped by a crescent of serous type of cells which secrete serous fluid only.
**Parotid-** is a serous gland.
**Submandibular gland-** is a mixed gland.
**Sublingual gland-** is purely mucous gland.
**Slide of serous gland (H& E)-** alveolar cells are stained deep pink in colour. The pyramidal alveolar cells have large round nucleus placed at base and pink

zymogen granules in apical part; showing basal basophillia ( bluish appearance) and apical eosinophilia (pink appearance) basal basophilis is due to RER which is present here to produce the secretary granules, apical eosinophilia is due to zymogen ( secretary) granules present there.  Small intralobular duct are clearly seen, lined by columnar epithelium which are stained still deeper.

**Slide of mucous gland (H & E stain)**-alveolar cells are stained very faint blue in colour. Smaller ducts are stained deeply. Mucous is usually removed during preparation of slide hence faint blue or vacuolated appearance of cells. Mucous fills most of the cytoplasm pushing nucleus to the base of the cells. Hence nucleus appears flattened at the base of the cell.

**Slide of mixed gland-** both the types of alveoli are seen. Mucous alveoli show serous demilunes or crescent.

4. **<u>EPIGLOTTIS</u>**

It is elastic leaf like structure situated at the opening of larynx. It guards the laryngeal opening during swallowing. So that no food particles enter the larynx.

**Histology-** centrally placed elastic cartilage, stratified squamous epithelium (moist type) is covering on both sides of epiglottis, mucous glands are situated underneath the epithelium in the lamina propria consisting of connective fibres.

## <u>ALIMENTARY SYSTEM</u>

Tube like structure beginning from oesophagus and ending at the anus.

**General structure** – consists of four coats, and they are form inside out.

1) **Mucous membrane-** made up of simple columnar epithelium, except the oesophagus and last portion of anal canal; a lamina propria of loose connective tissue, and a muscularis mucosae of smooth muscle fibres; lymphoid infiltration in lamina propria for defence line of G.I tract.

2) **Submucus coat-** made up of dense irregular connective tissue, containing large number of blood vessels, lymphatics and glands with lymphoid infiltration.

3) **Muscular coat-** made up of plain muscle fibres.

   **Inner-** circular layer.

   **Outer-** longitudinal layer.

4) **Serous coat-** peritoneal covering all throughout, except the oesophagus, and terminal half of rectum.

## 5. <u>OESOPHAGUS</u>

Musculomembranous tube like structure having-

1) Mucous membrane made up of stratified squamous epithelium which is non keratinised and is indented by the finger like projections of connective tissue of lamina propria. The mucous membrane shows several longitudinal folds which disappear on distension.
2) Muscularis mucosae is present in the lower part of oesophagus. It consists of longitudinal muscle fibres.
3) Sub mucus layer- loose connective tissue, oesophageal gland (mucous variety).
4) Muscular layer- upper one third of oesophagus has striated muscle; middle one third has mixed striated and plain muscle; and lower one third shows smooth muscle. Consists of inner circular and outer longitudinal layer of muscle fibres.
5) Outermost layer made up of dense fibrous tissue, containing lymphatic's & blood vessels. This forms the adventitia of the oesophagus.

**Slide of oesophagus:**
1) See stratified squamous epithelium moist variety.
2) Tubular structure with muscular wall.
3) Oesophageal glands in submucosa.

## 6. <u>STOMACH</u>

Dilated hollow musculo membranous bag has three different portions. Cardiac end, fundus with body and pyloric end.

**Mucous membrane-** thrown into longitudinal folds when the stomach is empty; called rugae. Stomach shows small openings along its inner surface on the mucous membrane called as gastric pits. Gastric pits are the openings of the gastric glands on the mucous membrane. The epithelium of gastric pits is columnar and mucus secreting but the cells appear empty as mucus is removed during processing. Gastric glands are branched tubular glands.

## GASTRIC GLANDS

- **Cardiac-** gastric pits are short. Tubular glands are long and lined by mucous cells. cardiac glands are present near the oesophageal opening of the stomach.
- **Fundic or main gastric-** gastric glands are simple tubular glands or branched tubular present in the lamina propria open on the gastric pits. Cells lining the glands are-
- **Mucous cells-** These secrete mucous. They are the large cells present in the neck region of the glands. Cytoplasm is clear and nucleus is flattened pushed to the base of the cells.
- **Parietal (oxyntic) cell-** these are large round and oval cells scattered among other gastric cells. They are large and stain very deep pink. These secrete hydrochloric acid and intrinsic factor.
- **Chief cell or peptic cells-** these cells secrete pepsin. They are numerous, present in basal part of gland. Cuboidal and faint basophilic. They secrete digestive enzyme including pepsin.
- **Argentaffin cell-** present at the base of the gland, small cells which lie between the chief cells and basement membrane thus they won't reach the lumen. They are stained with silver impregnation. Secrete gastric and serotonin.

The main gastric glands are present all over the stomach except cardiac and pyloric region of stomach.

## PYLORIC

Gastric pits are long and the glands are short, mainly consists of mucous cells.

No oxyntic cells. Gastric pits form two third of the membrane. While gland forms only one third part of the mucous membrane. They are present in the pyloric region of stomach.

**Lamina propria-** It is made up of loose areolar tissue, containing blood vessels, nerves lymphatic's etc.

**Muscularis mucosa-** are thin plain muscle fibres, situated deep to lamina propria, consisting of inner circular and outer longitudinal muscle fibres.

**Muscular layer-** Inner oblique layer, Middle circular layer and Outer longitudinal layer.

**Serous coat**- peritoneal layer, made up of simple squamous epithelium.


**Slide of stomach**-Identify all the layers of stomach inside out. Note the structure of mucous membrane of different parts of the stomach, as described above. Identify pits, glands, and look for oxyntic cells.


## 7. <u>SMALL INTESTINE</u>

**General of structure-** It has usual four coats.

**Peculiarities:** Mucus membrane is thrown in semicircular transverse folds in the upper half of small intestine. These folds have a cover of submucosa and they are permanent. They are called plicae semicircularies.

> **Epithelium-** Simple columnar epithelium, with striated border. Goblet cells are present. Paneth cells and argentaffine cells also present.
> **Intestinal glands-** these are the tubular invagination of the surface epithelium forming compound tubular glands in the lamina propria, known as crypts of lieberkuhn, (intestinal crypts). The glands are lined by undifferentiated cells which multiply and go along the surface of villi to replace the shed epithelial cell. Other cells like paneth cells are present in between. The surface of small intestine and the villi are lined by columnar cells which are specialised for adsorption as number of microvillus are present at the surface of the cells giving brush border appearance in H and E staining. Some goblet cells are present here and there on the surface epithelium.
> **Lamina propria-** composed of loose areolar tissue. Fills in core of villi and space in between the glands. Aggregation of lymphoid tissue is present in the form of solitary follicles or in large patches (peyer's patches in ilium).
> **Muscularis mucosae-** very thin layer of plain muscle arranged as inner circular and outer longitudinal layer. It forms the base for the villi, few muscle fibers from muscularis mucosae surround the lacteals here, helping the flow by contraction(milking action)
> **Submucosa-** Connective tissue. No gland present.
> **MuscularisExterna-** arranged in inner circular and outer longitudinal muscle fibres.

> **Serous coat-** peritoneal covering.

**Identification of slide of small intestine**
1) A tubular organ with muscular coats.
2) Presence of villi with lacteals.
3) Microvilli giving brush border appearance to epithelium.

# 8. <u>DUODENUM</u>

All the layer are as described above with few expectation.
1) Duodenal Glands (Brunner's Glands). These glands are present in submucosa. Their ducts pierce the muscularis mucosae and enter the lamina propria to open on the surface in the crypt of Lieberkuhn( intestinal glands).
2) Villi are not branching.

**Brunner's Glands-** They are compound tubulo alveolar glands present in the submucosa. The alveoli appear mucous secreting with flattened basal nuclei; their secretion is mucous and alkaline to neutralise acid coming to duodenum from stomach.

**Identification of the slide of duodenum**
Non branching villi.
Brunner's glands seen in submucosa; their ducts pass through muscularis mucosae and open on the surface.

# 9. <u>LARGE INTESTINE</u>
Comprises of caecum appendix, colon, rectum and anal canal general histological picture-
1) Layer are the same as that intestine.
2) Villi are not present. Glands numerous closely arranged, tubular.

3) Glands show very large number of goblet cells and columnar cells which adsorb 10 to 90% water and electrolytes. Mucous secreted by mucus cells as lubricant to facilitate the passage of faecal matter.
**Slide of large intestine.**

➤ Tubular organ.
➤ Mucous membrane does not show villi.
➤ Simple tubular glands present.
➤ Cells are mostly mucous cells (Goblet cells) lining the glands.

## 10.  APPENDIX

1) Blind diverticulum of the caecum.
2) Has same structure as that of large intestine, with following modifications
   a) Wall thick, lumen narrow.
   b) Lymphoid infiltration, all round in the lamina propria, submucosa, forming lymphoid ring (IMP)
   c) Muscularis mucosae, ill defined due to the lymphoid tissue.

**Identification of slide appendix:**
Tubular structure, mucus membrane not thrown into folds is seen in slide. Large number of goblet cells is seen in the tubular glands. See the lymphoid ring round about the tubular glands in the submucosa and lamina propria (IMP).

## 11. LIVER

Largest gland in the body. It is covered by peritoneum. Under the cover of peritoneum is the connective tissue capsule containing numerous elastic fibres (Glisson's Capsule). At the hilum, the fibrous capsule sends numerous septae (Trabeculae) and divides the substance of the liver into very minute, hexagonal structure known as lobule.

Lobules of liver are structural unit. Lobules are covered by capsule (Glisson's capsule). It is negligible in human.

> **Portal canal-** the space between the lobules are occupied by branches of hepatic artery bile duct and portal vein, enclosed in a network of connective tissue. This is a portal canal.

## LIVER LOBULE

A hexagonal lobule nearly 2 m.m. long and 1 m.m. wide.

1) **Parenchyma-** liver cells are large polyhedral cells, containing mainly glycogen and fat.

    The section, cells are seen arranged in single row (cords) in radiating manner from the central vein, which is present at the centre of the lobule. The liver cells are actually present in sheets or plates, which branch and anastamose. The spaces between the sheets are called sinusoids. The liver cell is actively secreting cell, hence organelles like mitochondria, RER, golgi apparatus are present. Some liver cells may show two or three nuclei. The liver produces bile.

2) **Sinusoids-** these are present in between the sheets of liver cells. They are lined by endothelial cells. Macrophages are present between endothelial cells of the sinusoids which show gaps. Macrophage cells are called kupffer's cells.

    The liver cells show microvilli on the sinusoidal surfaces. The macrophages cells are phagocytic in nature.

3) **Blood vessels-** Liver is richly supplied by blood. Hepatic artery and the portal vein are the main blood supply of liver.

    **These** vessels go in the connective tissue and branch out to smallest branches in the substance of the liver and lie in the canal at the periphery of the lobule from where these vessels open into sinusoids and pour in the mixed blood.(I.e. portal vein and hepatic artery).Blood flows from periphery to the centre in the hepatic lobule towards the central vein.

    **Hepatic vein-** central veins join together to form sublobular veins.

    Sublobular veins join together to form hepatic vein, which ultimately open into the inferior vena Cava.

4) **Bile canaliculi-** are the grooves between the opposed surface of the liver cells. These bile canaliculi carry the bile secretion from the centre of the lobule to the periphery of the lobule.The tight junctional complexes at

sides of bile canaliculi; golgi apparatus is present under the cell membrane opposing the bile canaliculus.

The bile ducts come as right and left hepatic ducts. They join together and with the cystic duct form the bile duct.

**Identification of the slide of liver.**

1) See the hexagonal liver lobules.
2) Central vein in the centre of the lobule.
3) Liver cells forming the hepatic cords, are arranged in radiating manner from the central vein, the radiating cells are large polyhedral cells with vesicular nuclei; may be binucleated. In between the liver cords are the sinusoids lined by endothelium and macrophage cells. the sinusoids contain mixed blood from hepatic artery and portal vein. The blood from periphery of the lobule towards the centre. Hence the cells in the peripheral part of the lobule get oxygen or nourishment more than the centrally situated cells.
4) At the periphery of the lobules look for the portal canal and identify the three structures lying in the portal canal. (The portal traid).

## 12.  GALL BLADDER

Hollow muscular membranous bag attached to the under surface of the liver. Wall of gall-bladder consists of three layers from within outwards-

1) **Mucosa-** It is lined by tall columnar cells with few mucous secreting cells scattered. These cells have the striated border( micro villi) for absorption of water there by concentrating bile which is stored here. The cells have microvilli to increase the surface of absorption. Mucous  membrane is thrown into many branching folds, which may anastamose giving reticular appearance.
2) **Muscular layer-** no definite arrangement of the muscle layer is found in the gall bladder wall. They are all irregularly arranged, with large connective tissue fibres arranged in between these muscle bundles.
3) **Serous coat-** layer of peritoneum, lined by flattened epithelium. Gall bladder stores and concentrates bile.

**Identification of the slide of Gall-bladder:**

A structure lined by mucous membrane thrown into many folds lined by tall columnar cells with brush border. No goblet cells seen.

No definite muscle arrangement.

Gall-bladder tissue will always be accompanied by a small piece of liver tissue.(IMP)

## 13. PANCREAS

This gland consists of two parts, exocrine part and endocrine part.

**Structure of pancreas:**

1) Connective tissue framework like that of salivary gland, forming a capsule. The whole gland has a connective tissue capsule.
2) Trabeculae divide the substance of the gland into many lobules. The trabeculae are the septa going from capsule into the substance of the gland.
3) Parenchyma of the gland is made up of two types of cells.

**Exocrine pancreas-** It is a compound tubule-alveolar gland. It is very vascular, blood vessels go through trabeculae. Alveoli are lined by serous type of cells which are pyramidal in shape. Cells show basal basophillia and apicaleosinophillia because of zymogen granules. Basal basophillia is because RER as cell is secretary cell. The secretion collects at the apical part as zymogen granules which stain pink with eosin. Intra-lobular ducts which join and form inter-lobular duct which form bigger ducts. These secretions of pancreas is poured by its duct into the duodenum. The large ducts are lined by tall columnar cell. Smaller ducts lined by cuboidal types of cell.

**The endocrine pancreas-** Groups of cells are present here and there in the exocrine part as islets of langerhans which is separated from exocrine alveoli by a network of reticular fibres. Rich capillary plexus is present in endocrine pancreas so that each cell comes in contact with the capillary to pour its secretion directly in the blood. Islet of langerhans) scattered throughout the pancreas. Sinusoidal vessels are present in these groups of cells. The cells are of different types.

**Alpha cells-** are present at periphery if islet and secretes glucagon.

**Beta cells** very numerous which are present in central part secrete insulin.

**Delta cells-** produce gastrin and somatostatin.

**P.P cells**- contains pancreatic polypeptide.
**The exocrine pancreas- -**

## IDENTIFICATION OF SLIDE OF PANCREAS:

a) All the alveoli of the glands are stained deeply as they are lined by serous types of cells.

b) Groups of cells (islets of Langerhans) are seen scattered here and there throughout the gland in lobules of the gland. They appear as small groups of cell faintly stained scattered here and there in the darkly stained alveoli of exocrine pancreas.

c) Identification of alpha and beta cell required special stains.

**QUIESTIONS:**

❖ What are the differentiating points between parotid glands and pancreas?

**TOUNGE**

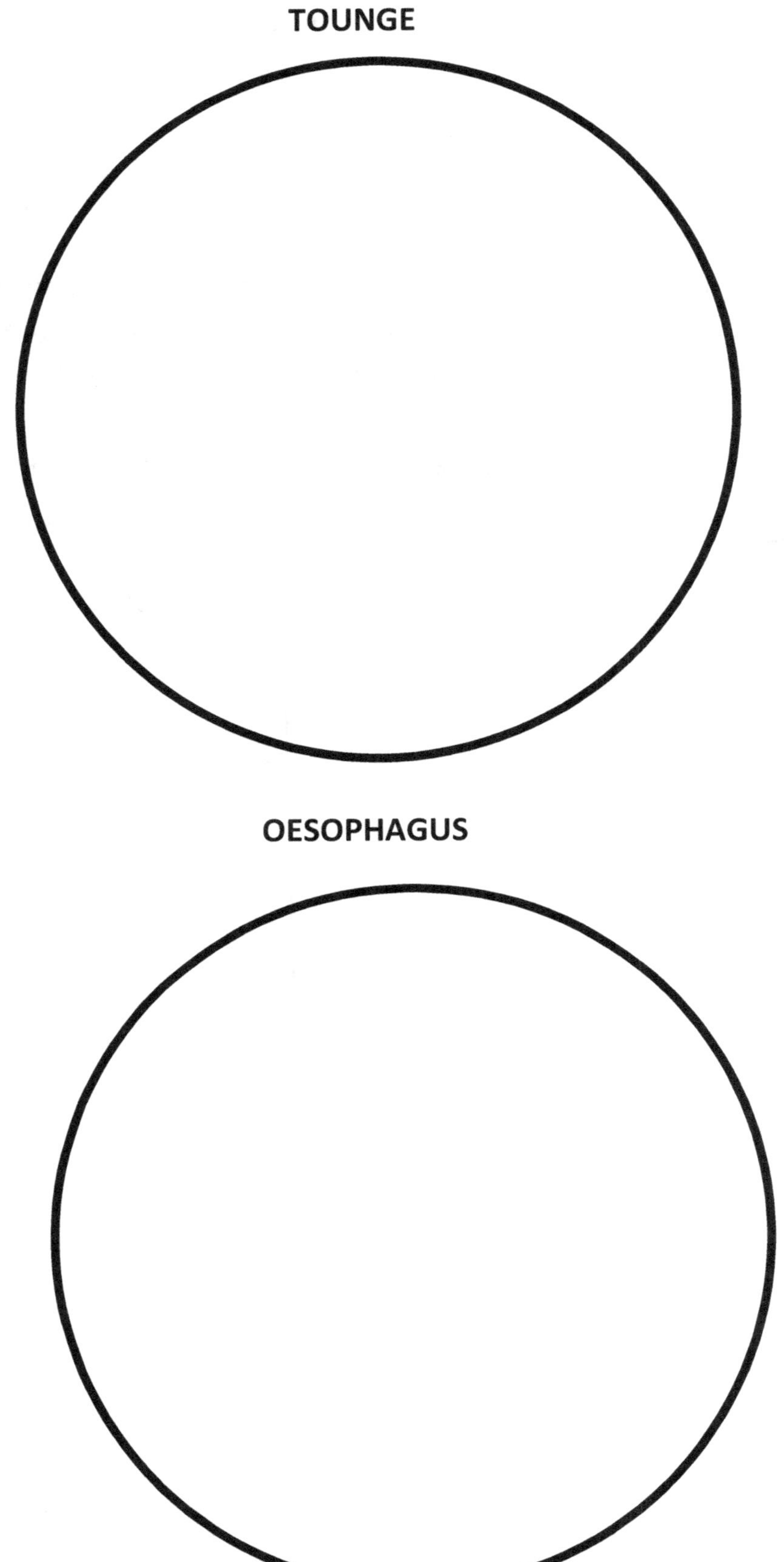

**OESOPHAGUS

## STOMACH (Fundic part)

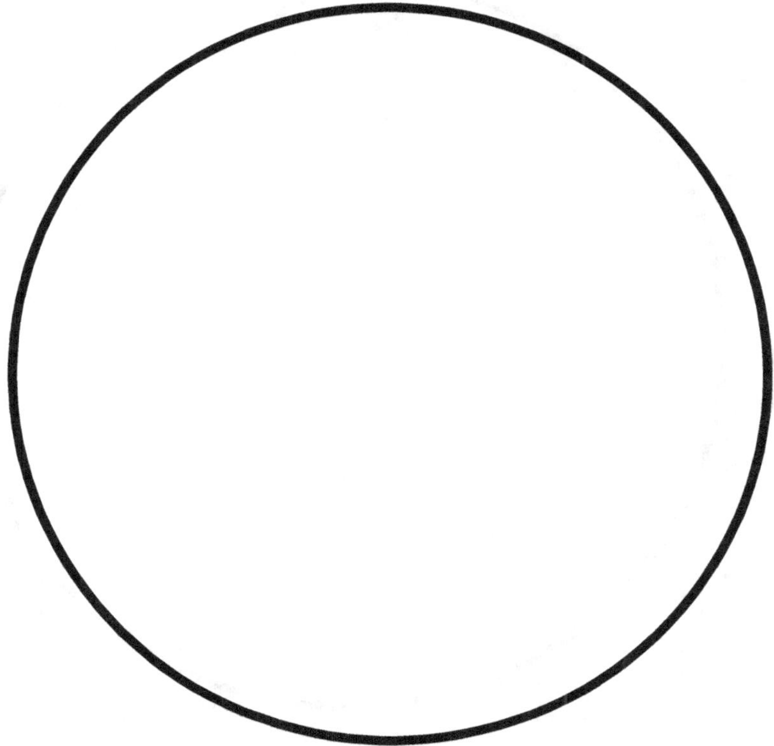

## STOMACH (Pyloric Part)

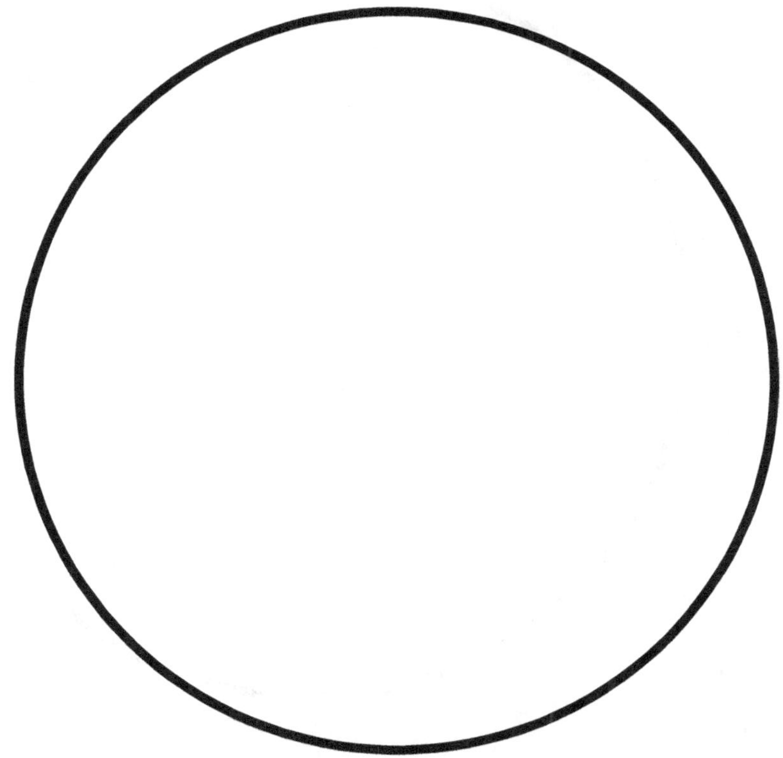

# DUODENUM

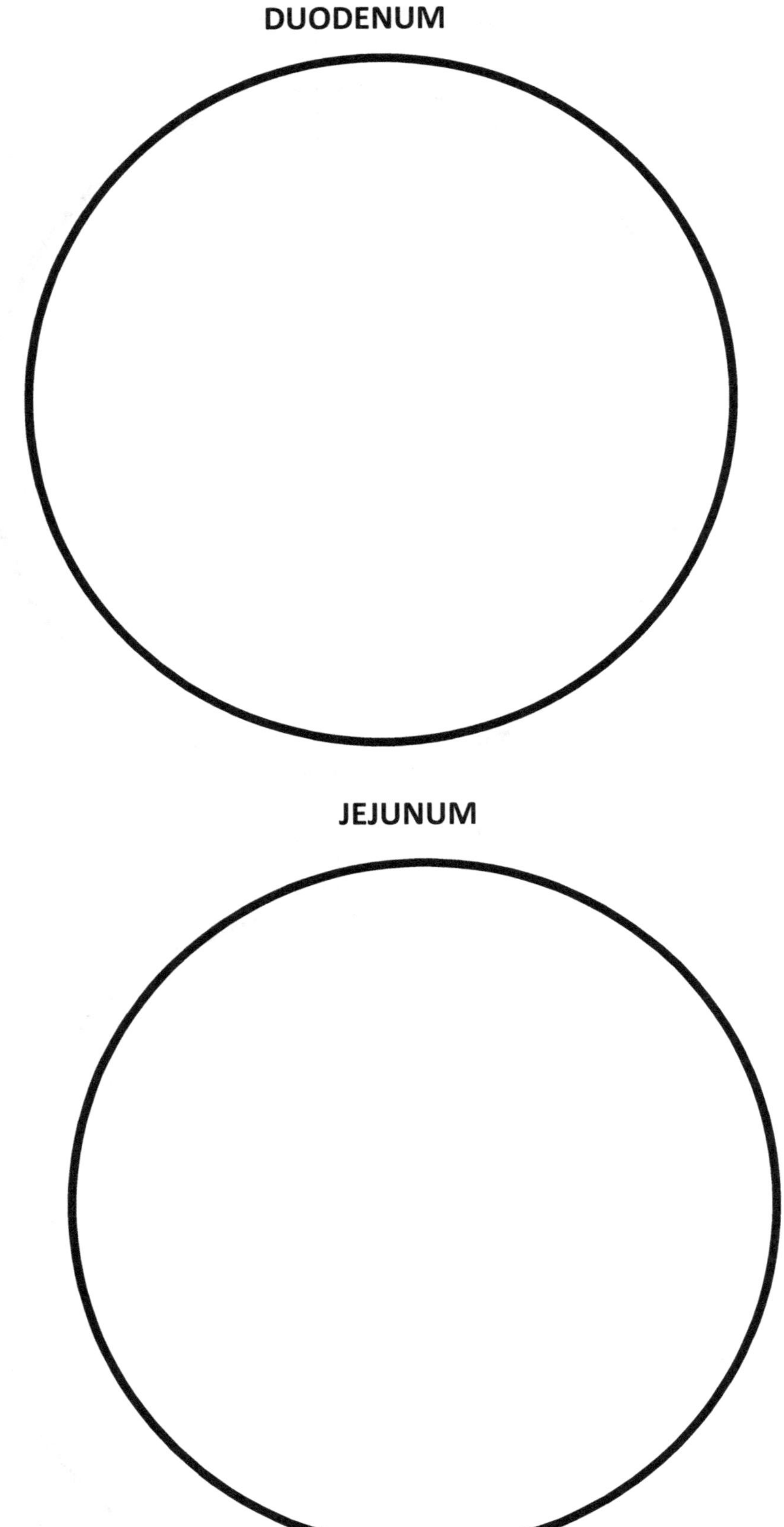

## ILEUM

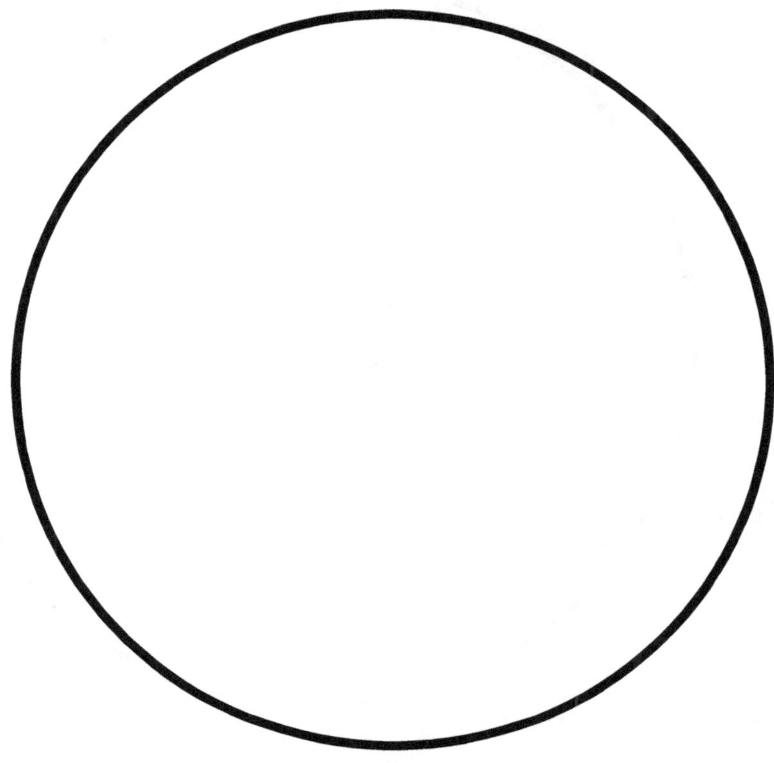

## LARGE INTESTINE

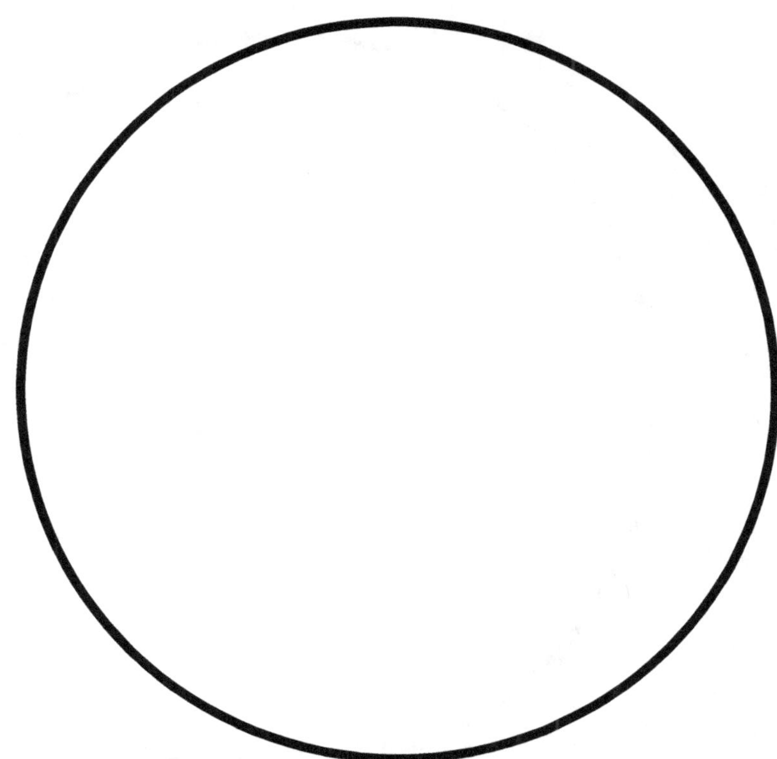

## APPENDIX

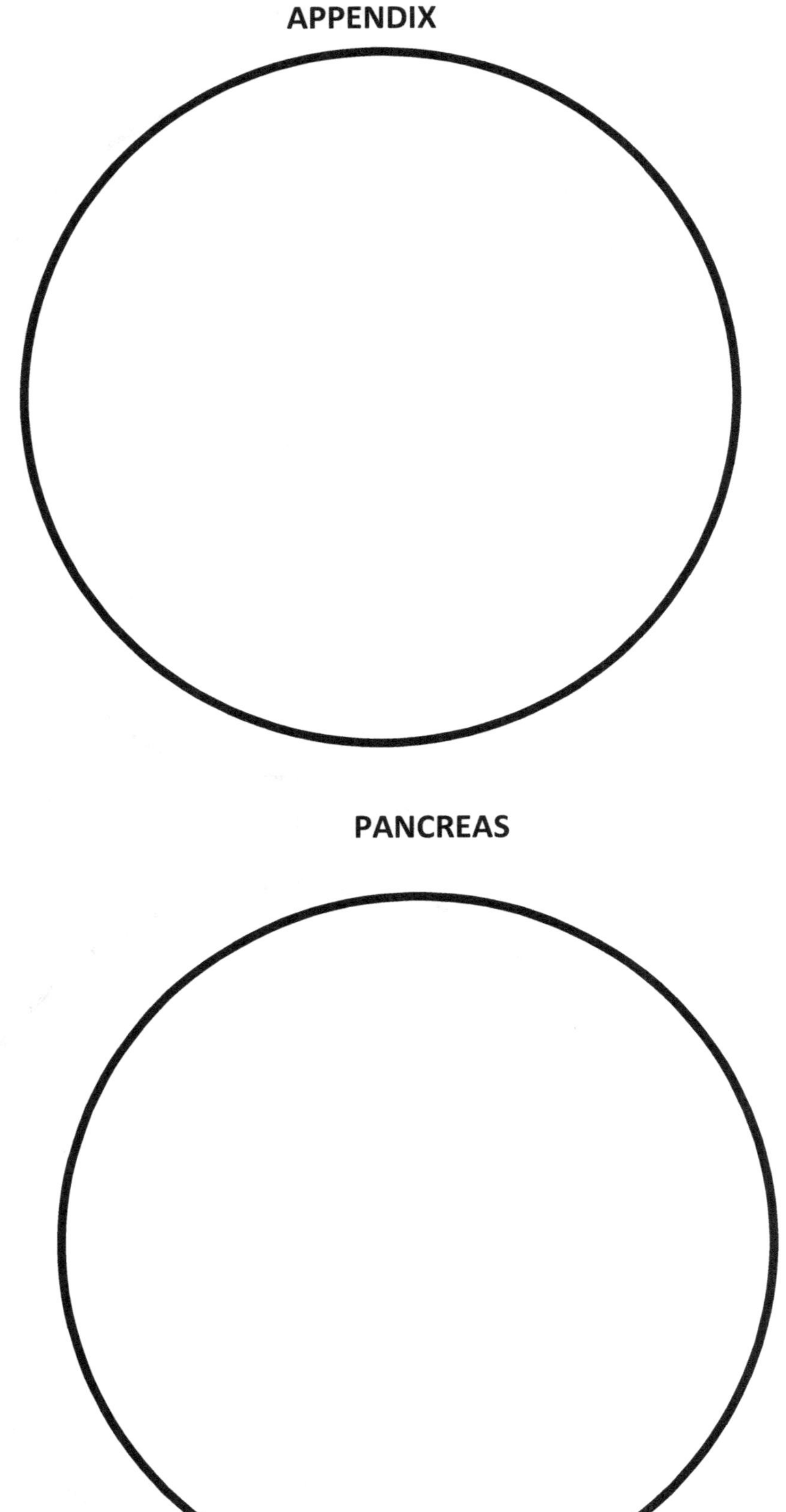

## PANCREAS

## LIVER

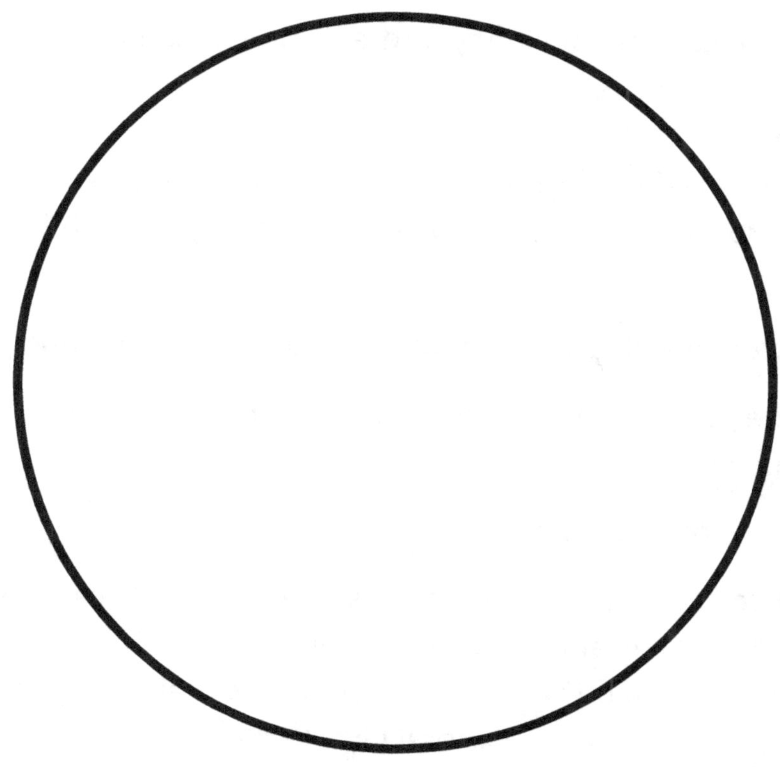

## GALL BLADDER

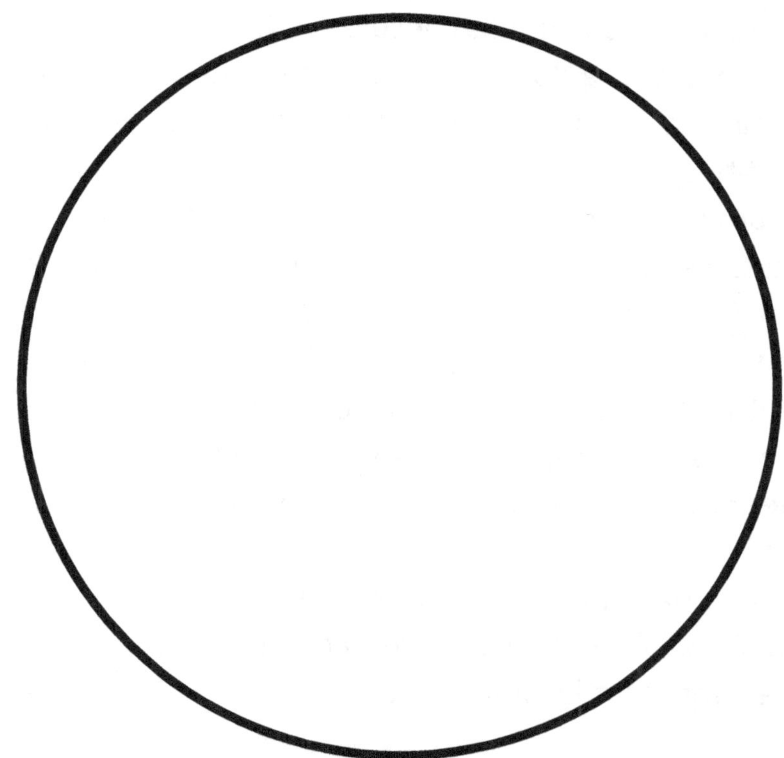

# CHAPTER NO. 13 - URINARY SYSTEM

This system consists of kidney, ureter, urinary bladder, and urethra.

1. **KIDNEY**
   In the intrauterine life the kidney is lobulated and during development these lobes unite to form one complete bean shaped organ. Each lobe is represented by the pyramid.

**Microscopic structure of kidney**- cortex of each kidney is composed as follows.

Nephron- is the functioning unit of the kidney, interstitial tissue in between the nephrons is much less.

**Nephron-** consists of various parts.

1) **Renal corpuscle-** consists of glomerulus and Bowman's capsules. A glomerulus is a rounded tuft of capillaries which are fenestrated. The afferent arteriole brings blood, it flows through the capillary bed and is drained by efferent arteriole. The glomerulus is covered up by visceral layer of Bowman's capsule. The visceral layer of Bowman's capsule consists of modified cells − podocytes, having foot like processes resting on the basal lamina of endothelium. This arrangement is to form a filtrate in the Bowman's capsule.
   **Bowman's capsule-** is a double layered epithelium cup. It has parietal and visceral layer. The parietal is formed **by simple squamous epithelium.** There is a space between the two layer which is continuous with the renal tube.
2) **Proximal convoluted tubule-** lined by cuboidal  cells, lying on the basement membrane. Cells have fine hair like structure (brush border). This brush border is due to very fine protoplasmic projections (microvilli) on the free surface of the cells seen with Electron micrography. PCT lies in the cortex. Lumen of proximal convoluted tubule is smaller as these cells are large. Nuclei widely separated.
3) **Descending limb-** structure is the same of convoluted tubule.
4) **Thin segment of loop of Henle-** it is lined by simple squamous epithelium. It lies in medulla.
5) **Ascending limb of Henle-** It is lined by cuboidal epithelium. It lies in medulla.
6) **Distal convoluted tubule-** These tubules are lined by cuboidal epithelium with basal nuclei and faintly staining cytoplasm. No brush border, Lumen of the

tubules – large. cells are smaller, so nuclei are close to each other, present in cortex. Distal convoluted tubule comes in contact with renal corpuscle at the vascular pole of glomerulus between afferent and efferent arterioles.

7) **Collecting tubules-** These tubules are lined by columnar epithelium. These tubules are the structures which form the medullary Rays. They are present both in cortex and extend into the medulla as well.

8) **Ducts of Bellini (papillary ducts)-** These ducts are also lined by tall columnar cells. They open at the apex of pyramid into the calyx minor.

### BLOOD SUPPLY OF KIDNEY- RENAL ARTERY AND RENAL VEIN

a) Renal artery enters the hilum and divides into 19-20 inter lobular branches which pass in between the pyramids towards the cortex.

b) Interlobar branches are out at right angle at the junction of the cortex and medulla of kidney. These branches are known is arcuate arteries. These arcuate arteries run parallel to the surface.

c) Arcuate arteries divide into smaller branches known as inter lobular arteries. The interlobular arteries run at right angle to the surface of the cortex.

d) Interlobular arteries give out afferent branches to the glomerular tufts.

e) Efferent branches from superficial glomerular tufts, from the capillary bed around convoluted tubules and then venules from there end in the interlobular veins.

f) Some of the efferent arteries form juxta medullary glomeruli, they pass straight into the medulla of the kidney, as known as Vasa Recta, which forms the capillary bed around the loop of Henle and collecting duct, veinae Recti start from the medulla which open into arcuate veins.

g) Arcuate veins join to form inter lobar veins.

h) Interlobar veins join to from renal vein which comes out of the hilum.

### 2. URETER

It is a musculo-membranous tube like structure, starting from the kidney and opening in the urinary bladder. The lumen of the ureter is star shaped due to longitudinal folds present in the mucous membrane. They disappear on distension.

It has three coats. They are from inside out-

1) **Mucous coat-** mucous membrane formed by the transitional epithelium supported on the lamina propria.

2) **Muscular coat** consists of two layer of plain muscle fibre, inner longitudinal and outer circular; a third longitudinal layer present outside in lower part of the ureter.

3) **Outermost Fibrous coat-** made up of loose connective tissue and adipose tissue.

**Identification of the slide of kidney:**

a) See the rounded structure containing tufts of capillaries surrounded by the Bowman's capsule.( glomeruli)

b) Tubules are cut across which can be seen with their lining epithelium. identification of different types of tubules is different but can be identified by brush border, large cells and nuclei away from each other ( proximal convoluted tubule) and small cells no brush border and nuclei closely placed ( distal convoluted tubule).

c) Medullary Rays can be seen cortex. Glomeruli and the tubules cut across at various sections is the identification feature of the slide of kidney.

**Identification of the slide of ureter-**

Small tubular lined by Transitional Epithelium is the point of identification of the ureter, the lumen appears star shaped.

## 3. <u>URINARY BLADDER</u>

Structure of the urinary bladder is the same as that of ureter except that the bladder has got the three muscle coats; inner layer of longitudinal muscle fibres, middle layer of thick circular muscle fibres and outer layer of longitudinal muscle fibre. The transitional epithelium shows 4-5 layers of the cells when not distended. The muscle contracts during emptying of bladder. Hence name detrusor of the muscle. The layer of muscle coat not clearly demarcated. The muscle forms circular sphincter vesicae at the junction of the bladder and urethra.

**Identification of slide of bladder-**

A small piece of an organ which is lined by transitional epithelium is the slide urinary bladder with smooth muscles oriented in different direction.

## 4. URETHRA

Urethra is the membranous passage for urine, surface of the mucus membrane are opposed to each other except during passage of urine.

**URETHRA**

| **1.Male urethra** | **2) female urethra** |
| --- | --- |
| This is covered by thick masses in all the three parts | It is small and 1 ½" long. |

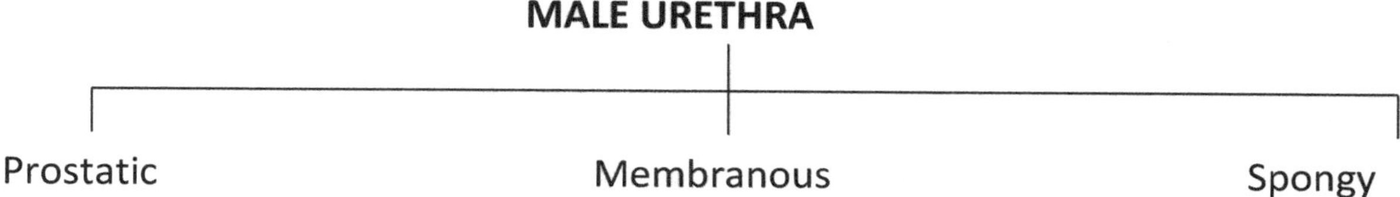


Before going on to the study of urethra, we will study of the male genital organ: penis.

**Structure of the corpora cavernosa and spongiosum:**

It consists of large number of lacunar spaces lined by endothelium and surround by connective tissue and muscle fibres.

The penile part of the urethra is situated in the corpus spongiosum. It is terminal part which is situated in the glans penis and is lined by stratified squamous epithelium. The rest of the part of the urethra is lined by stratified columnar epithelium, except the proximal part from internal sphincter up to the opening of the ejaculatory ducts; it is lined by transitional epithelium.

At many places the mucous membrane invaginates in the sub-mucosa and these invaginations are known as lacunae of morgagni. At the base of the lacunae these urethral glands (glands of litter) are present which are lined by tall columnar epithelium.

**Female urethra**- It is short and measured 1 ½ inch length. It is lined by stratified squamous epithelium near the opening. It has few lacunae and the middle portion of the urethra is lined by stratified columnar epithelium.

**QUESTIONS:**
1) What is nephron? What are different parts?
2) What is the function of brush border of the first convoluted tubule?
3) What is transitional epithelium? Give its function? What are umbrella cells?
4) What is juxta medullary glomerulus? Does it function like other glomeruli?
5) What is the blood supply of medulla of kidney?
6) How musculature of ureter and the urinary bladder is arranged?
7) What is juxta-glomerular apparatus? What is its function?

## KIDNEY (low power)

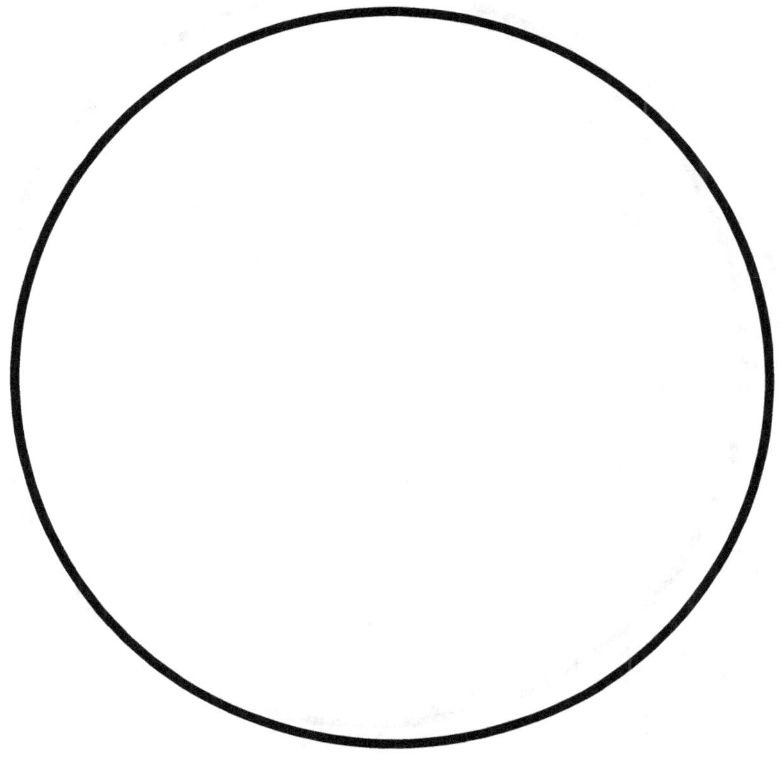

## KIDNEY (High power)

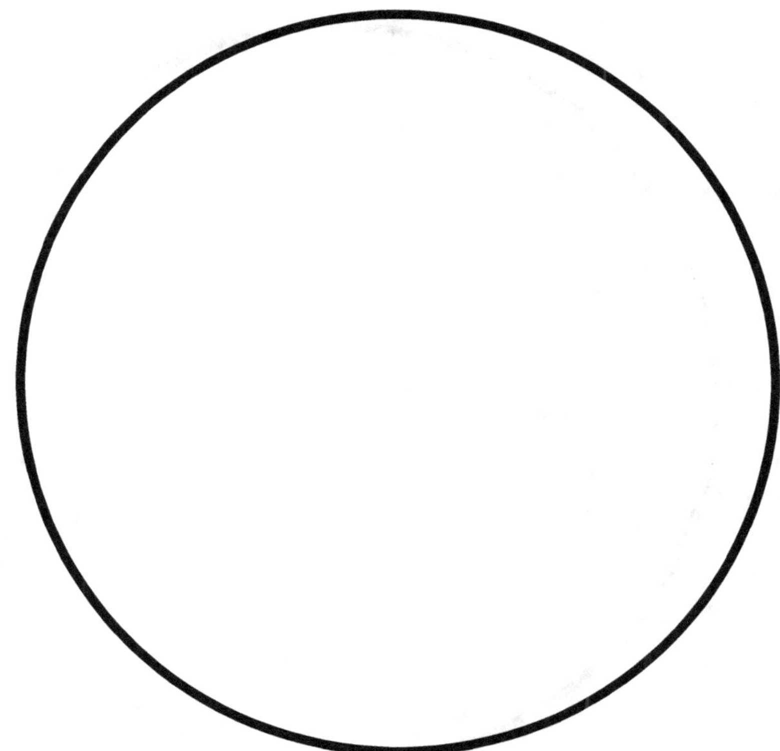

## URETER

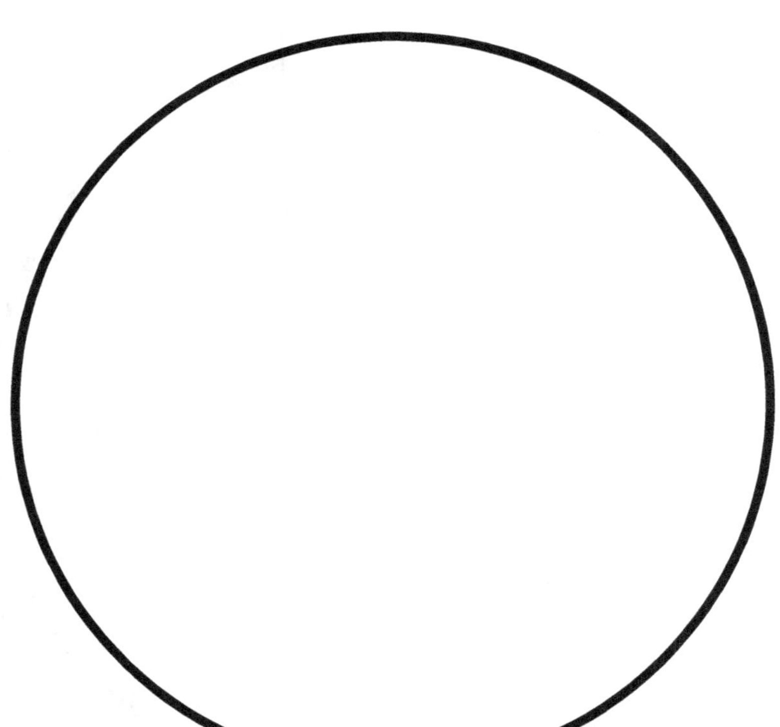

## URINARY BLADDER

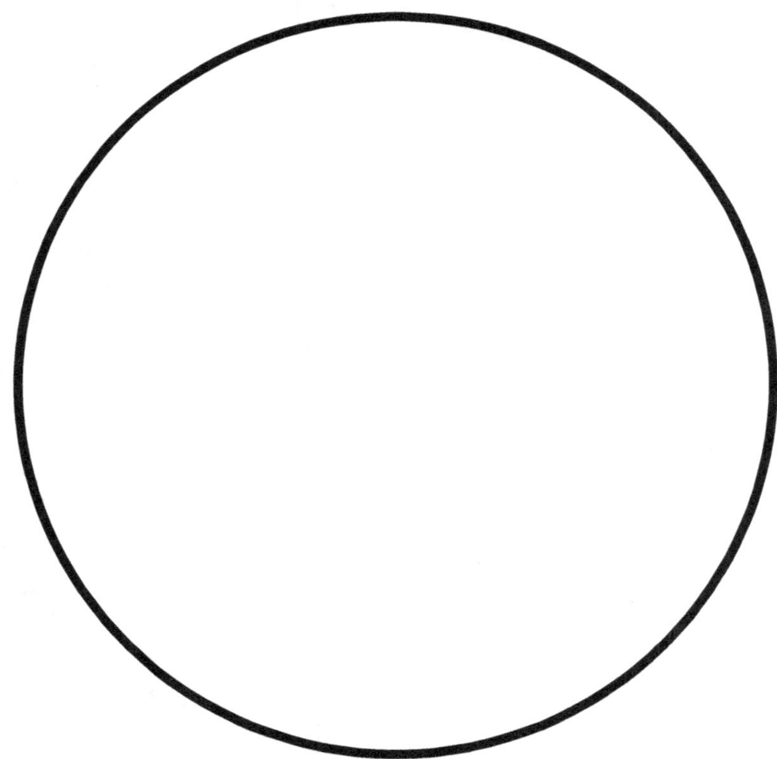

# CHAPTER NO.14  Male Genital System

It consists of Testis, epididymis, vas deferens, seminal vesicles, ejaculatory ducts and prostate.

## 1.  TESTIS

Testis is oval; it is covered by thick fibrous covering forming the tunica albuginea. From posterior part of tunica albuginea, septa traverse in the substance of the testis forming number of lobules.

Each lobule contains one or more seminiferous tubules which form the site for formation of sperms. The space between the seminiferous tubules is filled by loose connective tissue, blood vessels and lymphatics. In the intertubular space groups of interstitial cells of Leydig are present which secrete testosterone.

The seminiferous tubules open into the straight tubules which enter the network of tubules called rete-testis. From rete-testis efferent ducts pass to the head of the epididymis. This is the passage for sperm formed in seminiferous tubules. Testosterone being hormone is released in blood directly.

Histology of testis is the study of the seminiferous tubules.

➢   **SEMINIFEROUS TUBULES**

They are highly convoluted. Hence in the cut section appear as various shapes. These tubules are covered by connective tissue coat on the outside.  These tubules are lined by stratified layers of spermatogenic cells and the sustentacular cells (cells of sertoli).

**Spermatogenic cells-** These are the sex cells in various stages of development up to the formation of spermatozoa. There are the several layers of these cells. They are supported on the basal lamina. The basal layer is of spermatogonium which forms the primary spermatocyte and spermatogonium by mitosis. From primary spermatocyte, secondary spermatocyte develops by meiosis and form spermatids. Spermatids form sperms which cling to the sertoli cells in the lumen. The process comprises of spermatogenesis and spermiogenesis.

1) **Spermatogonia-** are large cells resting on the basal lamina; undergo mitosis to produce more spermatogonia and primary spermatocytes (46 chromosomes).
2) **Primary spermatocyte-** large cell with spheroidal nucleus lies on the inner side, undergo meiosis to produce secondary spermatocytes with half the number of chromosomes. (23 chromosomes)
3) **Secondary spermatocytes-** smaller in size and are short lived immediately undergo meiotic division to form spermatids (23 chromosomes).
4) **Spermatid-** small round cell near the lumen. Undergo changes in shape to form sperm. This process is called spermiogenesis.
5) **Sustentacular cells-** These are the cells which support the spermatogenic cells and also provide nutrition to the growing spermatozoa. They are large cells with branching process to which the spermatogenic cells cling. They rest on basal lamina protrude into lumen.
6) **Interstitial cells-** (leydig cells) these are the large round cells responsible for the production of the testicular hormone (testosterone). These cells are present in groups in the intertubular connective tissue. They stain faint pink with eosin. The seminiferous tubules have old cells on outer side of basal lamina. This produces peristaltic contraction of the tubule.

### 2. <u>EPIDIDYMIS</u>

It is greatly coiled tube forming a mass of convoluted tube situated on the upper part of the testis, fitting like cup. It is comma shaped, having a head body and tall becoming continuous with the vas deferens. It stores sperms and help maturation of sperms.

**Structure-** tube covered by connective tissue and plain muscle sheet, mucous membrane lining of the tube is tall columnar epithelium, all the cells having nearly the same height so that the inner margin of the lumen is regular. Clumps of the sperms seen in lumen.

The columnar cells of the tube have got hair like no motile processes (stereocilia). They are the microvilli.

❖ **Identification of the slide of testis:**
**1)** Seminiferous tubules cut across at various sections.

2) Rounded structure (tubules) lined by stratified layers of the spermatogenic cells in various stages of development. Newly formed sperms clinging to sertolli cells.
3) Intertubular connective tissue seen.
4) Leydig's cells seen in the intertubular connective tissue as large polyhedral cells.

❖ **Identification of the slides of epididymis:**
1) Tubes cut across at various sections.
2) Typical tall columnar epitheliumcells having the same height, thus making the lumen a regular one. Cells show large microvilli (stereocillia)
3) Epididymis will always be accompanied with a small tissue of testis.

### 3. <u>VAS DEFERENS</u>

It is a tube like structure starting at the tail of epididymis. It is a musculo-membranous tube like structure.

**Section of the vas Deferens:**

Mucous membrane shows pseudo-stratified columnar epithelium supported on basement membrane. A lamina propria of connective tissue is seen at outside.

**Muscular coat-** it has three muscle coats.
1) Inner thin longitudinal muscle fibres.
2) Middle very thick circular muscle fibres.
3) Outer thick longitudinal muscle fibres.
   Outer most layer of adventitia of connective tissue is present.

❖ **Identification of the slide of vas deferens:**

A thick muscular tube like structure lined by pseudo stratified epithelium; very thick middle muscular coat is the identification of vas deferens.

## 4. PROSTATE

It is a fibro musculo glandular organ, situated at the neck of urinary bladder. It is enclosed in fibro elastic capsule. It produces secretions rich in enzymes (acid phosphatase), prostaglandins, citric acid.

Capsule sends in septa and this fibromusculoelastic stroma lies in between the alveoli of the prostatic glands.

**Prostatic Gland-** consists of ducts and alveoli.

**Ducts-** Ducts have irregular lumen. 15- 20 ducts open into the prostatic part of the urethra. They are lined by columnar epithelium.

**Alveoli-** mucus membrane is thrown into large and small folds, lining epithelium is cuboidal or columnar. Basal cells are present in between the columnar cells.

**Prostatic concretions** (corpora amylacea)- These are the aggregated granular masses of prostatic secretion, arranged in lamellated form. These are more number in old age. They are made up of coagulated protein and nucleic acid.

### ❖ <u>Identification of prostate:</u>

1. Very thick fibromusculoelasticstroma in between the alveoli of the gland.

2. Epithelium lining the alveoli is thrown into many folds.
3. You may see the portion of the prostatic part of the urethra in the section.
4. Prostatic concretions may be seen.

Note- This slide is always to be differentiated from the slide of passive mammary gland mucous membrane of alveoli of mammary glands is not thrown into folds.

# TESTIS

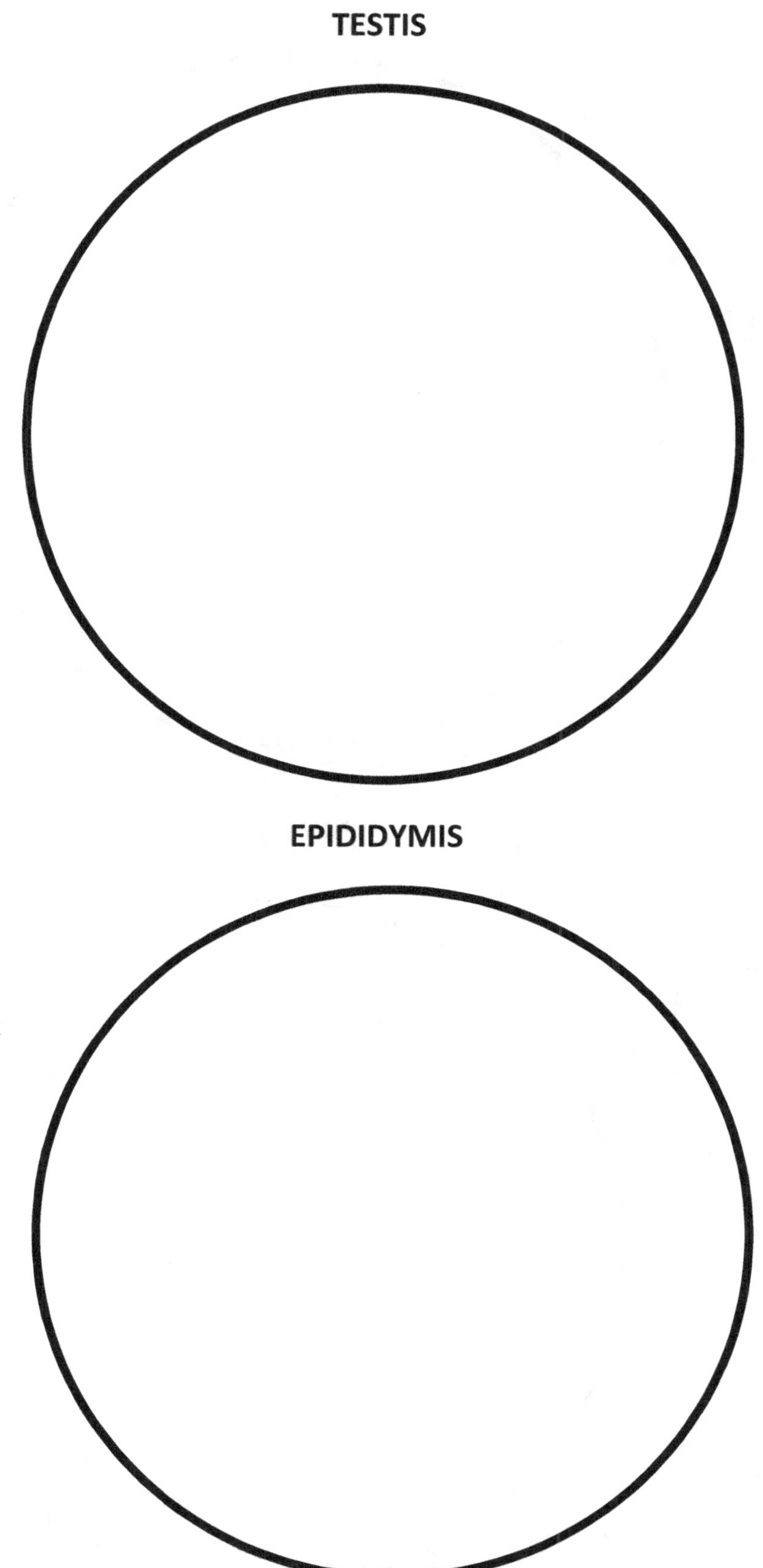

# EPIDIDYMIS

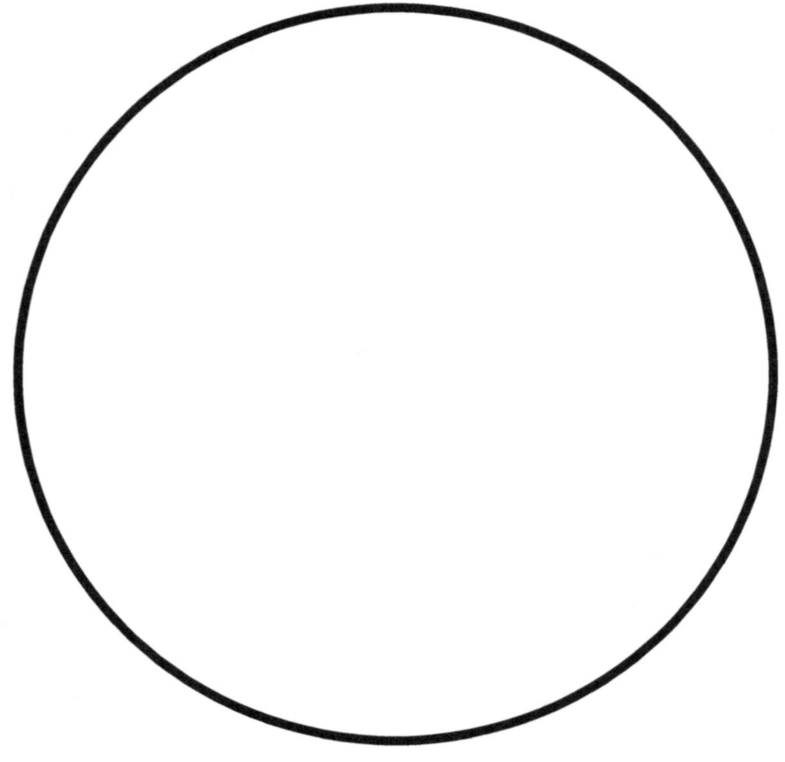

**PROSTATE**

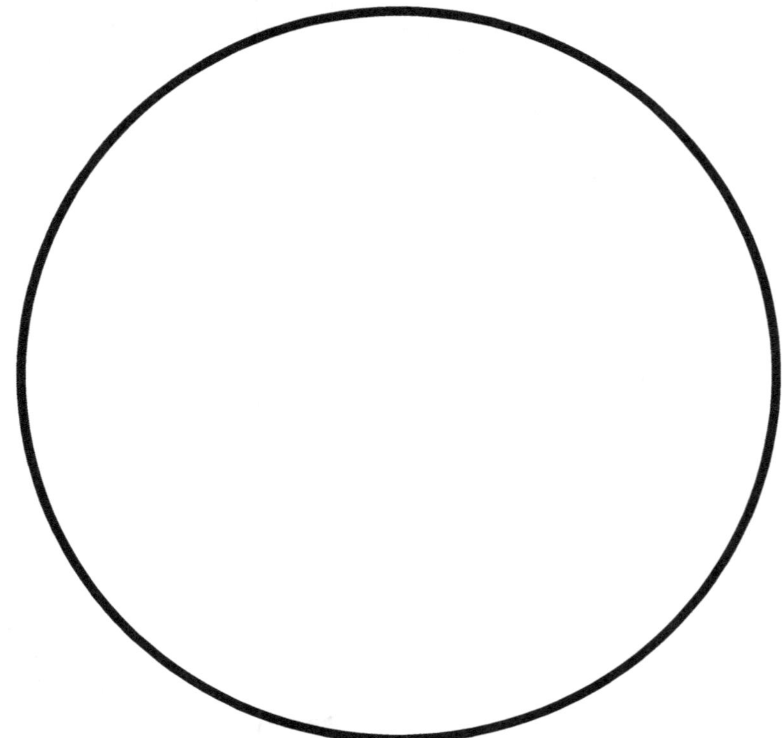

# CHAPTER NO. 15  -  Female reproductive organs

Female genital organs comprise of the following organs:

**External genitalia**

1)  Vulva and vagina   2) Accessory glands- Mammary glands
    Placenta- is also included in the chapter

**Internal genitalia-** these are situated in the pelvic cavity. 1) Ovaries 2) Uterine tubes  3)uterus

# 1. <u>OVARY</u>

Ovary is a female gonad. It produces ova, the female sex cells (gametes) and female hormones, the oestrogen and progesterone. Through the production of hormones ovary produces cyclical changes in the uterine mucosa.

Ovary is a small oval structure nearly 3cm. in diameter present in the angle between uterine tube and uterus on posterior aspect.

**General structure:** Surface is covered by mesothelial cells, known as germinal epithelium. Connective tissue stroma lines in between groups of cells known as ovarian follicle.

The ovary shows cortex and medulla arrangement.

**Cortex-** Immediately deep to germinal epithelium is the tunica albuginea which is condensation of connective tissue. There is a stroma of cortex consisting of reticular fibre and fusiform mesenchymal cells. Scattered in this stroma are the ovarian follicles at different stages of development.

**Medulla-** The central core of the ovary consists of connective tissue, with numerous blood vessels.

**Oogenesis:**

The sex cells in the female are present at birth. There is no further increase in the number of cells by multiplication. The cells are called oogonia which forms primary oocyte. Primary oocyte has 46 (diploid) chromosomes.

Primary oocyte undergo first meiotic divisions and form two unequal cells; the large is the secondary oocyte containing 23 chromosomes and the other very small cell called first polar body which also contains 23 chromosomes. The secondary oocyte undergoes second meiotic division and form two unequal cells. Large one containing 23 chromosomes in the mature ovum and very small cell called second polar body. Thus one primary oocyte gives rise to one mature ovum only.

**Ovarian Follicles:**

1) Oocyte or sex cell surrounded by a single layer of flattened cells called primordial follicle.
2) Oocyte grows and flat cells proliferate. This is called primary follicle.
3) Primordial follicle are about 7,00,000 in one ovary at birth.
4) These lie dormant till the age of puberty and number decreases uo to 40,000. The oocyte is a large cell with eccentric nucleus and prominent nucleolus. It is surrounded by a homogeneous membrane called zonapellucida.
5) At puberty these follicles undergo further development and change into one mature follicle every month, releasing one ovum from ovary per month at ovulation.

## DEVELOPMENT OF OVARIAN FOLLICLE

Cells of primordial follicle proliferate and form many layers of cells. Cavities appear in these masses of cells. These cavities join together and form big cavity filled with follicular fluid, this is called secondary follicle. At this stage the follicle contains large follicular cavity and the ovum with some cells is pushed to one side. This ovum is attached to the wall of the cavity by surrounding cells. When this follicle grows and attains maturity, ovum is set free in the abdominal cavity which is surrounded by the small radiating columnar cells known as corona radiate.

The cells of stroma surround the follicle and form theca. The theca interna produce oestrogen. The theca cells and follicular cells are separated by basal membrane.

**Corpus Luteum–** When the ovum is shed out, same ovarian follicle collapses to form corpus luteum. The wall becomes folded. The cells proliferate and differentiate to become large cuboidal cells containing lipid.

Corpus luteum secretes hormone progesterone. The follicular cells and theca cells become large and accumulate lipid called lutein.

**Atresia of the follicle** – Normally at birth, 7,00,0000 primordial follicles are present in an ovary. Every month follicles start growing, but only few reach maturity and only one ruptures at ovulation. The rest then undergo degeneration. This process is called atresia of follicles.

**Identification of the slide of ovary :**

1) Look for the primordial follicles scattered throughout the field. Each of the follicles will show an ovum.
2) See the fibrous stroma round each follicle.
3) See the ovarian follicles. In some ovum it is seen and in some it is not seen. This absence of ovum may be due to the section passing through a plane which did not cut ovum

## 2. <u>UTERINE TUBE</u>

It is a musculomembranous tube like structure. Hence we have to study the following layers.

- **Mucous membrane**. It is thrown into very many folds especially in ampulla of the tube. It is lined by ciliated columnar epithelium. There are also present other type of cells which are glandular in nature.
- **Muscular coat** consists of inner and outer longitudinal layer.

**Identification of the slide of uterine Tube:**
1) Musculomembranous tube.
2) Mucous membrane thrown into many folds.
3) Mucous membrane lined by ciliated columnar epithelium. Slide of uterine tube be confused for seminal vesicle because of multiple mucosal folds. But cilia of uterine differentiated.

# 3. <u>UTERUS</u>

Pear shaped organ very thick muscular walls. It has a body; the cervix; the structure of the two is different. The uterus has outer peritoneal covering. Then a thick muscular coat called the myometrium and inner mucosal layer called endometrium.

- ➢ **Muscular coat-** three different muscular coats, but coats cannot be differentiated clearly. Large amount of connective tissue is present in between the bundles of muscle fibres.

  **Outer layer-** longitudinal and circular coats.

  **Middle layer-** circular and oblique.

  **Inner layer-** longitudinal and circular. In pregnancy uterine muscle increases in length many time of their normal length. After delivery the muscle fibres again come to normal size (Imp). The increased in length and size of uterine muscle during pregnancy is by hypertrophy of muscle fibres. Large number of uterine blood vessels, nerves and lymphatics are present in the connective tissue which is present in the myometrium.

- ➢ **Endometrium-** Endometrium is divided into functional and basal layer. The functional superficial layer is shed at the menstruation and then undergoes proliferation and secretary function during reproductive period of a female under the hormones oestrogen and progesterone of the ovary. The endometrium consists of the surface epithelium and a stroma. The surface epithelium consists of columnar epithelium ciliated at places. The stroma is formed by loose spindle shaped cells. Number of glands is present in the stroma which opens on the surface. The uterine glands are striated during the proliferative stage of menstruation. But become enlarge and coiled like cork-screw in the secretary phase of menstruation. The functional layer is shed at menstruation and the whole of endometrium is rebuilt by basal layer during proliferative phase of menstruation.

**Identification of the slide of uterus:**

1) Thick muscular walled organ lined by tall columnar epithelium.
2) Tube like glands in various sections which are cut and the portions of the glands placed one below other. (cork screw like gland).
3) Different layers of muscle fibres cannot be identified separately.

## 4. MAMMARY GLAND

Deep to the skin of mammary gland there are glandular masses separated by connective tissue. The granular tissue consists of 15 to 20 lobes. Each lobe has a coiled duct lactiferous duct which dilates before opening on the nipple. This dilatation is called lactiferous sinus. The structure of mammary gland varies in female at different periods of life.

1) **Before puberty**- the mammary gland consists mainly ducts. The duct system proliferates after puberty under the hormonal influence of oestrogen and progesterone.

2) **During pregnancy** the ducts proliferate and proper alveoli are formed which start secreting milk towards the end of pregnancy.

3) **During lactation** there is marked increased in the alveoli and comparatively the connective tissue and fat becomes less.

4) **After lactation** ceases, gland resumes the resting phase and after menopause it atrophies.

### Structure of gland:

Glandular part consists of compound tubuloalveolar gland. Alveoli drain into intralobular ducts. Intralobular ducts open into lactiferous ducts and lactiferous sinus.

10 to 13 lactiferous ducts open on the surface nipple.

**Mucous membrane-** Alveoli are lined by columnar epithelium.

**Myoepithelial cells-** large cells with finger like branching process, present between the alveolar cells and basement membrane. They connect and thus help in removal of milk from the alveoli into ducts.

**Small ducts-** are lined by single or double layer or cuboidal epithelium.

**Terminal duct-** lined by stratified columnar epithelium.

**Connective tissue-** large amount of fibrous connective tissue stroma lies in between the ducts and the alveoli, so also fat.

Mammary gland is ectodermal in origin. At birth the gland has no alveoli but has solid cords of cells which canalise at puberty.

## 5. PLACENTA

Placenta is discoid organ which attaches the foetus to the uterus of the mother for nutritional, respiratory and excretion purpose. It carries nutritive materials from mother's blood to the foetus, and the waste products from the foetus to the mother blood.

Placenta secretes hormones progesterone and oestrogen.

**Structure of villi**

1) **Primary villi**- consists of projections of cytotrophoblast and syncytiotrophoblast.
2) **Secondary villi**- are formed when the mesodermal core enters the villi.
3) **Tertiary villi**- are formed when the blood vessels grow into the secondary villi. These are formed on the 21 days of pregnancy.

**Floating villi look like branching creeper in water tank of the maternal blood pool.**

Section of villius will show.

1) Outer syncytiotrophoblast layer
2) Inner cytotrophoblast layer. Disappears after the fifth month of pregnancy.
3) Inside this you will find the mesenchymal core; containing (foetal) blood vessels.

**Placental Barrier-** The foetal blood in the foetal blood vessels of the chorionic villi is separated from the maternal blood from the maternal blood pool by the following structures.

1) Endothelium of the foetal blood vessels (capillary).
2) Basement membrane of the foetal capillary.
3) Mesenchymal core of chorionic villi.
4) Syncytiotrophoblast.

The placental barrier becomes thinner by disappearance of cytotrophoblast, widening of the foetal blood vessels and thinning of the mesodermal core in the later months of the pregnancy for better exchange of nutrients, hormones and gases between the mother and growing foetus.

**Identification of the slide of placenta-**
1) Note the large number of villi cut transversely. Which may show circular or oval shape.
2) Note the blood vessels in the mesodermal core of the villi.
3) You will find large number of the empty spaces. They are maternal blood sinuses. During sectioning, blood has been washed off.

# UMBILICAL CORD

It is the cord like structure containing umbilical blood vessels which carry nutrition to the foetus from the mother's blood. One end of the cord is continuation of the placenta where it is attached to it, the other end enters the foetus through the umbilicus of the foetus.

**Structure of umbilical cord-** transverse section of the cord shows embryonic connective tissue (Wharton's jelly) which is covered by flattened layer of the cells. (embryonic ectoderm). Wharton's jelly consists of stellate cells with branching processes in a thick mucoid ground substance. Inside that jelly like mass are the umbilical Arteries and umbilical Veins.

## OVARY

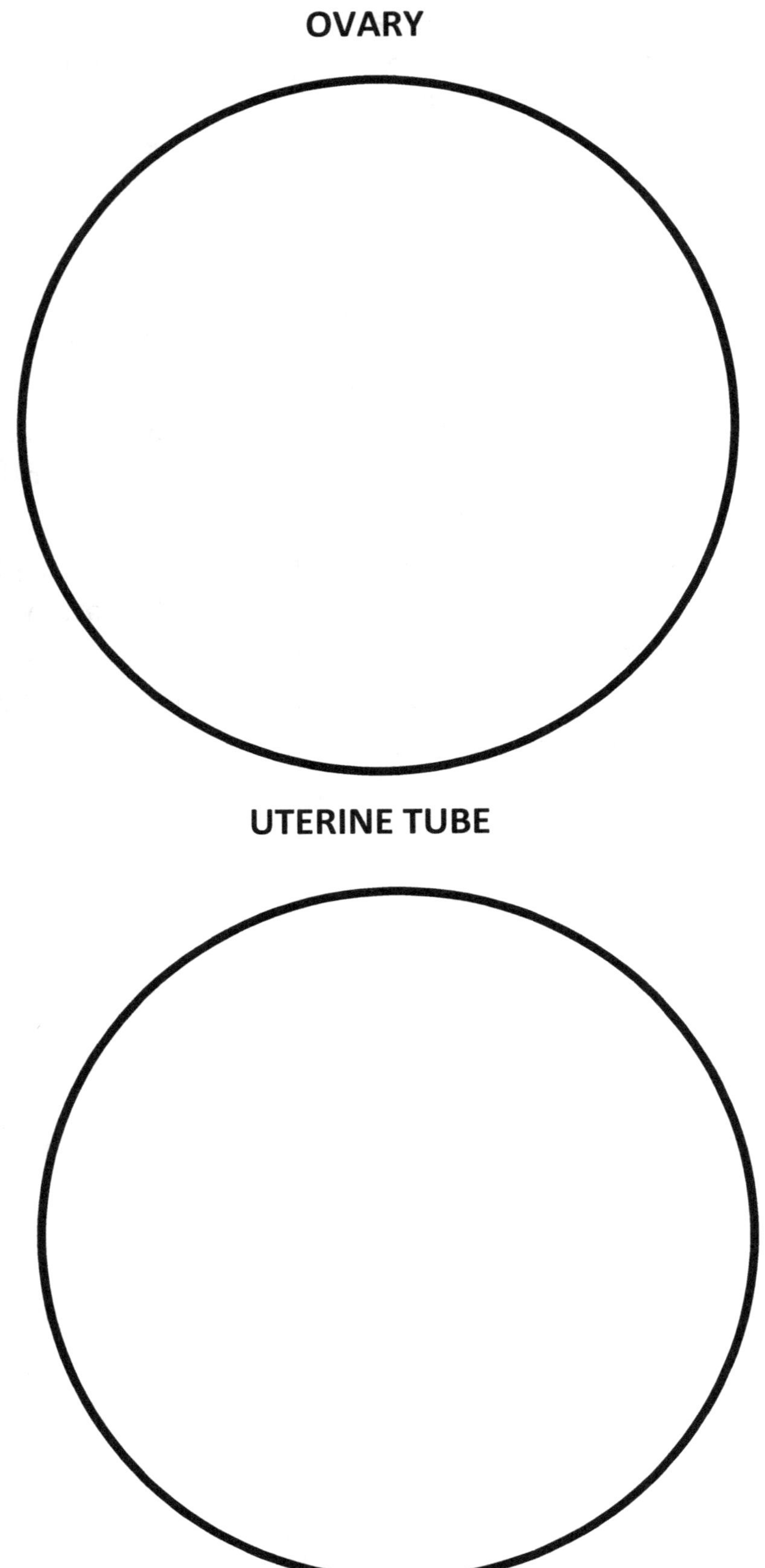

## UTERINE TUBE

## UTERUS (Proliferative)

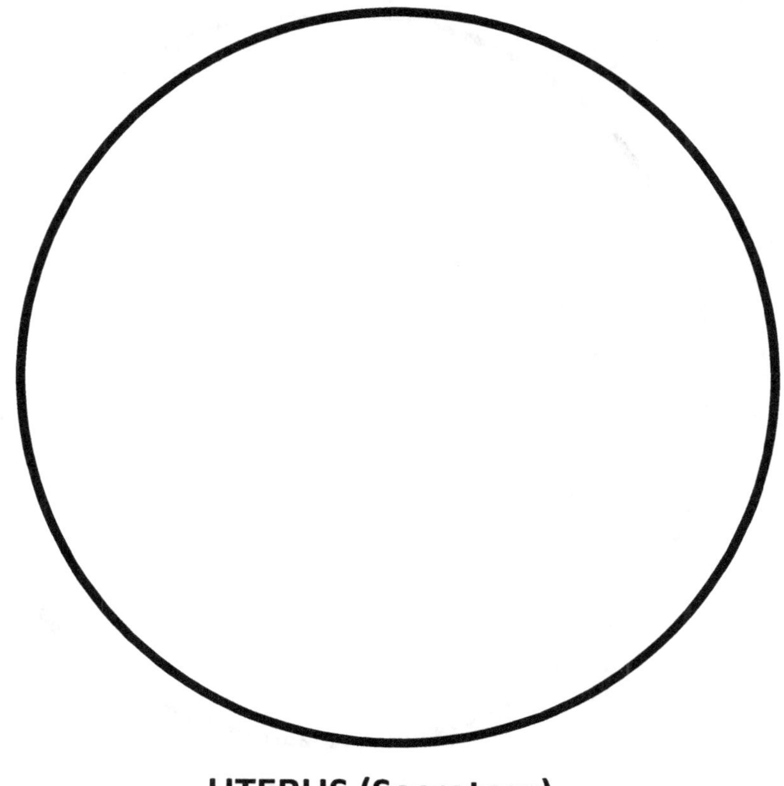

## UTERUS (Secretory)

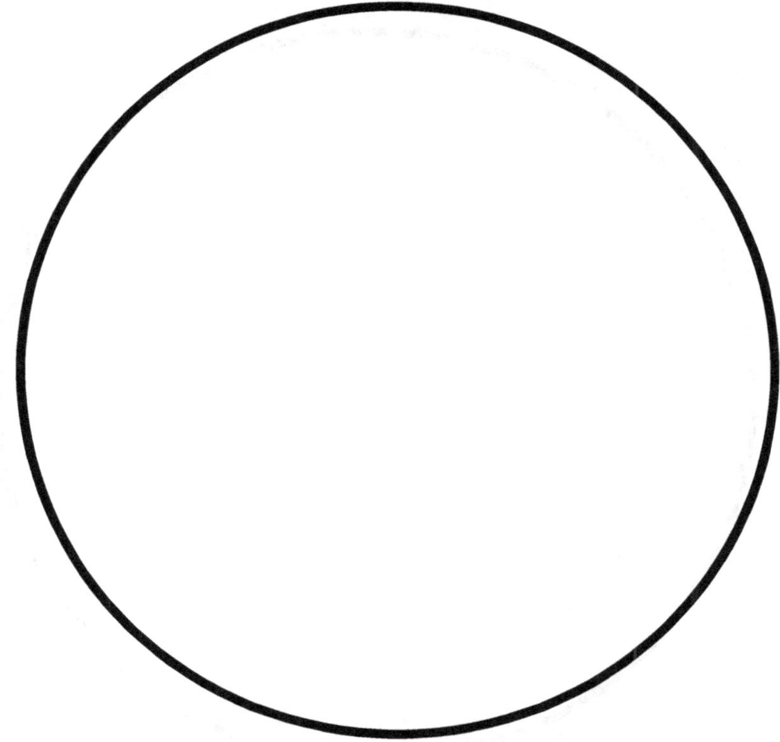

## MAMMARY GLAND (Active)

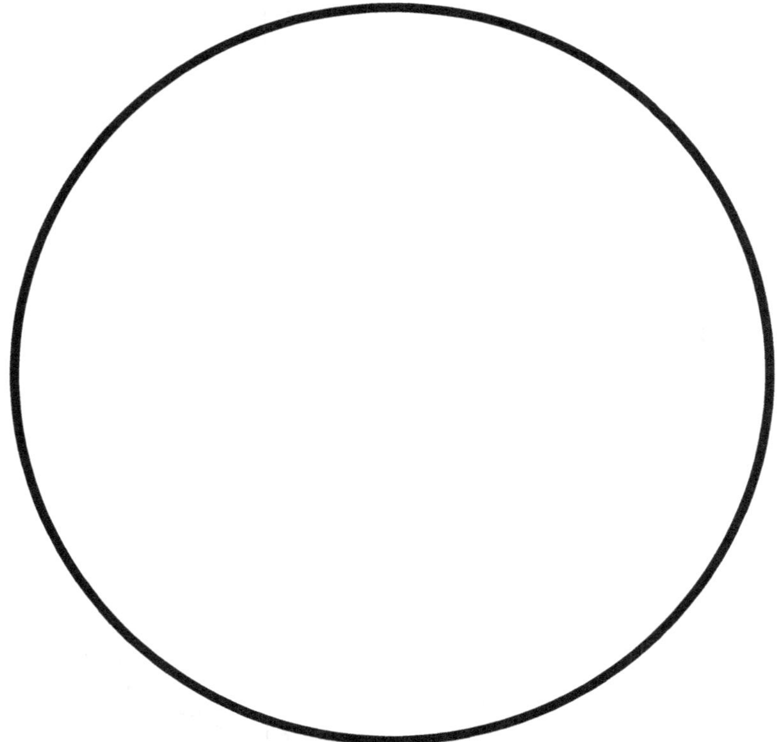

## MAMMARY GLAND (Passive)

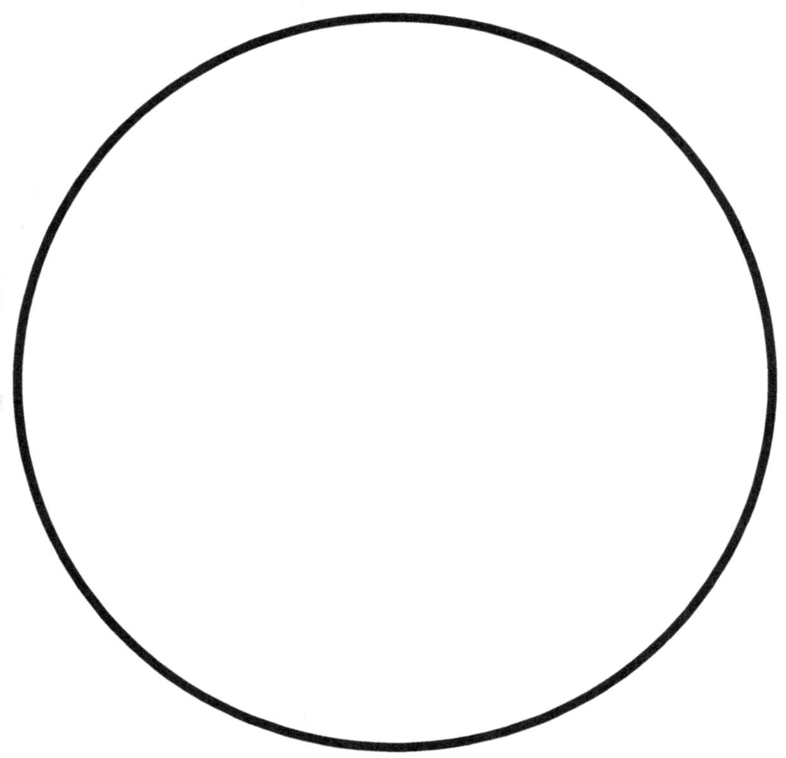

## PLACENTA

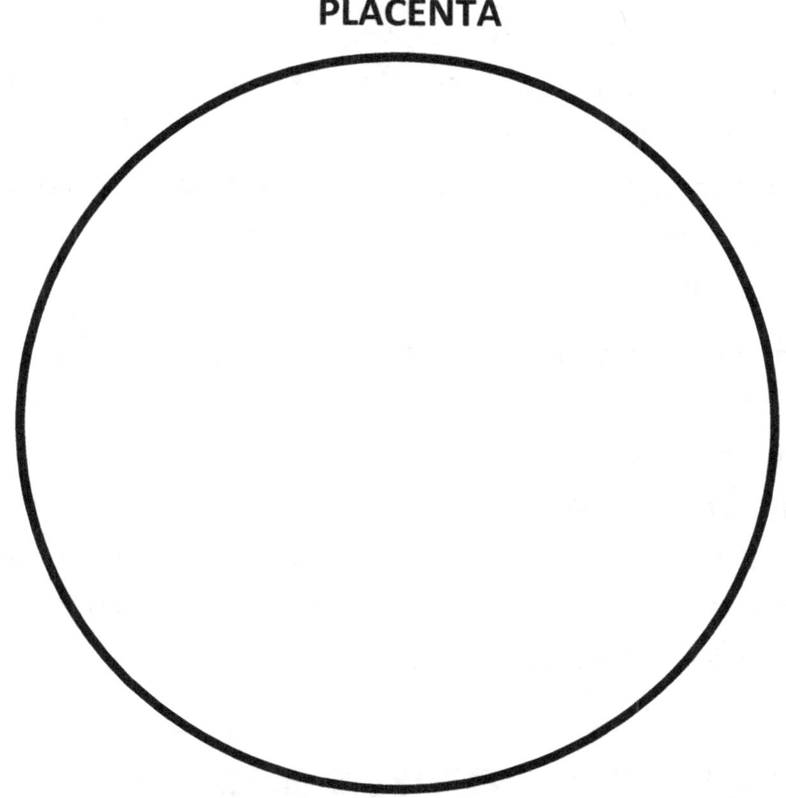

# CHAPTER NO. 16-   ENDOCRINE GLAND

The endocrine tissue consists of cells which produces secretions that are poured directly into the blood circulation as the tissue is ductless. Hence the endocrine glands have rich blood supply and each cell of the gland must come in contact with a blood capillary of sinusoid. The autonomic nervous system controls the internal environment and metabolism of the body.

**Distribution of endocrine tissue:**

1) Endocrine cells are present in organs having other functions e. g. Islets of Langerhans in pancreas, interstitial cells of leydig in Testis and corpus luteum of ovary. Hormones are also produced by kidney; Thymus and placenta. Liver is also described as endocrine gland.

2) Isolated endocrine cells present in the epithelium of gut. (APUD)

3) Endocrine organs which are having endocrine function only e.g .: Pituitary, Adrenals, Thyroid, Parathyroid and Pineal.

## 1. <u>PITUITARY GLAND (HYPOPHYSIS CEREBRI)</u>

**Development** - Develops from oral ectoderm and Neuroectoderm.

From oral ectoderm - Glandular part of the gland, the anterior Lobe develops. (Adenohypophysis).         .

**From Neuroectoderm** - i.e. from the floor of IV ventricle the posterior lobe (Neurohypophysis) develops.

**Divisions of Pituitary Gland**

| Lobes | Parts |
|---|---|
| **Anterior Lobe** (Adenohypophysis) | • Pars Distalis <br> • Pars Tuberalis <br> • Pars Intermedia |
| **Posterior Lobe** (Neurohypophysis) | • Pars Nervosa <br> • Infundibular stalk <br> • Median Eminence |

## Adenohypophysis or Anterior Lobe

**1) Pars Distalis-** This part is composed of cords of various types of cells separated by sinusoids. The cells are Chromophobe cells and the others are chromophil cells. Which are Acidophils and Basophils. The chromophobe cells do not contain granules. While the chromophil cells contain granules which take acid stain like eosin or basic stain like Haematoxylin. With special staining techniques the acidophils and basophils are subdivided into several other types. The cells responsible for production of particular hormone can also be recognised by immuno fluorescence technique. The following cells are recognised by this technique.

## ACIDOPHILS

- **Somatotrophs** - Secrete somatotrophic hormone which controls body growth.

- **Mammotrophs** - Secrete mammotrophic hormone which stimulate growth and activity of the female mammary gland during pregnancy and lactations.

- **Corticotrophs** - Produce ACTH which stimulate the secretion of adrenal cortex. Actually staining properties of this type of cell are midway between acidophils and basophils. So they are also included in basophils as well.

## BASOPHILS

- **Thyrotrophs -** Produce thyrotrophic hormone which stimulate the activity of thyroid gland.

- **Gonadotrophs** - Produce FSH & LH. These follicle stimulating hormone and Luteinizing hormones have action on male and female gonads.

**In the female** - The FSH stimulates growth of ovarian follicle and thus the production of oestrogen from follicle. The LH stimulates maturation of corpus luteum and thus secretion of progesterone from it.

**Chromophobe cells**. - The acidophils and basophils when become degranulated are called chromphobe cells.

   2) **ParsTuberalis** - Cells are mostly undifferentiated, few acidophils and basophils are present.

   3) **Pars Intermedia** -It is poorly developed in Human brain and it consist of colloid vesicles. These are remnants of pouch of Rathake. The cells secrete

(MSH) melanocyte stimulating hormone which causes increased pigmentation of the skin.

## Posterior Lobe (Neurohypophysis)

It consists of nerve fibres and cells called pituicytes. The nerve fibres which are nonmyelinated are axons of the neurons of supraoptic and Paraventricular nuclei of Hypothalamus. The secretion of these neurons is called neurosecretion which is carried by the axons to the posterior pituitary. At the ends of the axons in the posterior pituitary the secretions are  stored as Hering bodies which are located near the blood vessels. The neurosecretions are hormones oxytocin and ADH (Anti duretic hormone) also called vasopressin. They are released into the circulation, as and when needed, from the Hering bodies:

The ADH has effect on kidney which controls re-absorption of water from distal convolute tubules. The oxytocin has action on smooth muscle of uterus and mammary gland producing contraction of smooth muscle. Thus the hormones of posterior pituitary are produced in the Hypothalamus and are carried and released in blood stream in the posterior pituitary. The pituicytes are small cells which resemble neuroglial cells. Only nuclei are seen in the slide stained with H &E.

**Control of Secretion of Adenohyposis** - It is by Hypothalamus producing releasing hormones for each of the pituitary hormone.

**Practical Hints** - Section of the glands shows two distinct portions, anterior lobe and posterior lobe. See the two distinct portions by moving the slide from one end to other.

The portion full of cells is the anterior lobe. The portion stained very faint, and which shows large number of fibres is in the posterior lobe. Chromophobe and Chromophil cells are faintly stained in H & E preparation. The chromophils show acidophils (pink) and basophils (Blue) faintly stained by eosin and Haematoxylin respectively.

## 2. <u>THYROID GLAND</u>

It consists of two lateral lobes and a portion joining the two lobes which is known as isthmus.

**Structure of the gland** - The gland is enclosed in a fibroelastic capsule. Capsule sends in trabeculae which divides gland into lobules. Lobule has stroma of reticular fibres containing large number of blood vessels.

Lobule comprises of large number of Thyroid Follicles. The follicles vary in size and are surrounded by connective tissue and large number of blood vessels. The follicles are lined by follicular cells and contain homogeneous material called colloid.

**The Follicular cells** - Lining the follicles; vary in shapes depending on the activity of the follicle. When the follicle is actively secreting hormone; the lining cells are tall columnar and colloid is negligible in the follicle. With average secretary activity the cells are cuboidal with moderate amount of colloid in- the follicles. When the follicles are in resting phase the cells are flat & follicle is full of colloid.

**Colloid Material** - This material is secreted by the follicular cells and this accumulates in the vesicles. This material consists of a conjugate protein material (Thyroglobulin). Colloid contains iodine which combines with thyroglobulin. It forms a homogeneous material stained pink with eosin. Thyroxin is the active principle of the hormone which regulate the metabolism of the body. Apart from follicular cells there are Parafollicular cells or 'C' cells (clear cells). They are large polyhedral cells present between follicular cells and basement membrane. They do not reach the lumen of the follicle. They secrete Thyro-Calcitonin which lowers the serum calcium level. Thus it has opposite action to that of parathormone.

**Identification of the slide of Thyroid:**
1) Follicles of varying sizes lined by cuboidal epithelium.
2) Reticular fibre network round the vesicles.
3) Colloid material in the cavity of vesicles.


## 3. <u>PARATHYROID</u>

These are the two pairs of small bodies attached to the posterior side of the lateral lobes of the thyroid gland. The gland is covered by fibrous capsule, which sends in septa and divide the gland into lobules.

Lobules consist of solid masses of the parenchymal cells. Parenchymal cells form cords of cells arranged near walls of the capillaries. Which are present in the reticular stroma of the lobules. There are two types of cells present in the parenchyma.

1)Chief Cells.
2)Oxyphil Cells.

**Chief cells** - Much more numerous than oxyphil cells. These cells appear as small cells with vesicular nuclei. (They resemble lymphocytes). Cytoplasm is mildly acidophilic. The chief cells produce hormone parathormone which increase the serum calcium level by resorption of calcium from bones by osteoclasts .

**Oxyphil Cells** - Are absent in young and appear after puberty. They are large cells with cytoplasm darkly stained pink by eosin. Nucleus is dark and small. The function of oxyphil cell is not known.

**Identification of the slide of Parathyroid:**

1)General picture of a densely packed cellular organ;
2)Groups of pale and oxyphil cells are seen.
3)This tissue is always accompanied by a piece of thyroid gland.

# 4. <u>SUPRARENAL GLAND</u>

These are two in number, situated on the upper pole of the kidney. It has two regions cortex and medulla.

**Structural Plan** - Capsule, Trabeculae.
**Cortex** - made up of epitheloid cell columns. Cortex is larger than medulla.
**Medulla** - Made up of loosely arranged cells around the sinusoids.

**Cortex** - Cortical parenchyma is disposed of as columns of cells separated by the fibrous trabeculae, containing blood vessels and nerves.

Three zones are seen in the cortex.

1) ZonaGlomerulosa - Cells small polyhedral with basophilliccytopolasm and deeply staining nuclei arranged in groups of inverted "U" - shape structures.

2) ZonaFasciculata - Cells are large polyhedral. Cytoplasm contain lipid which is washed away during processing hence giving vacuolated appearance to cell. Cytoplasm basophillic with vesicular nuclei. These cells contain large amount of Vit 'C'.

3) ZonaReticularis - Cells are large polyhedral like Zona fasciculata. Cytoplasm

is often eosinophilic. Cells are arranged in cords anastomosing with large number of sinusolds in between.

**Medulla** - Is very small in man but is much bigger in lower animals. Demarcation of cortex and Medulla is not very well marked. It has irregular margins.

Medulla consists of polyhedral cells arranged in groups or cords around the sinusoids.

Groups of cell are supported by elastic fiber network.

**These cell gives rise to Chromaffin Reaction** - i.e. cells stain yellow with Potassium dichromate solution. This reaction is absent with cortex. The cells of medulla have affinity for chrome dyes.

Apart from these cells there are sympathetic Ganglion cells also.

## Functions:

### Cortex –

**1) Zona Glomerulosa** - Produces mineralocorticoids i.e. aldosterone and deoxycorticosterone. They influence the water and electrolyte balance of the body.

**2) Zona Fasciculata** - Produces glucocorticoids i.e. cortisone and cortisol, these hormones have effect on carbohydrate metabolism. They also decrease antibody response and they have anti inflammatory effect.

**3) Zona Reticularis** - This zona produces some glucocorticoids and sex hormones, both oestrogen & androgens. Suprarenal cortex is essential for life. Removal or destruction of cortex leads to death unless hormones are supplied artificially.

### Medulla:

Functionally cells of suprarenal medulla are like post ganglionic sympathetic neurons. They produce adrenaline and noradrenalin which increase heart rate and blood pressure.

## Identification of the slide of Suprarenal:

1)See the cortex and medulla and identify them.
2)See the arrangement of cells in the cortex and identify the three zones.
3)Identify Medulla - See the group of cells arranged round about the sinusoids.

## PITUITARY

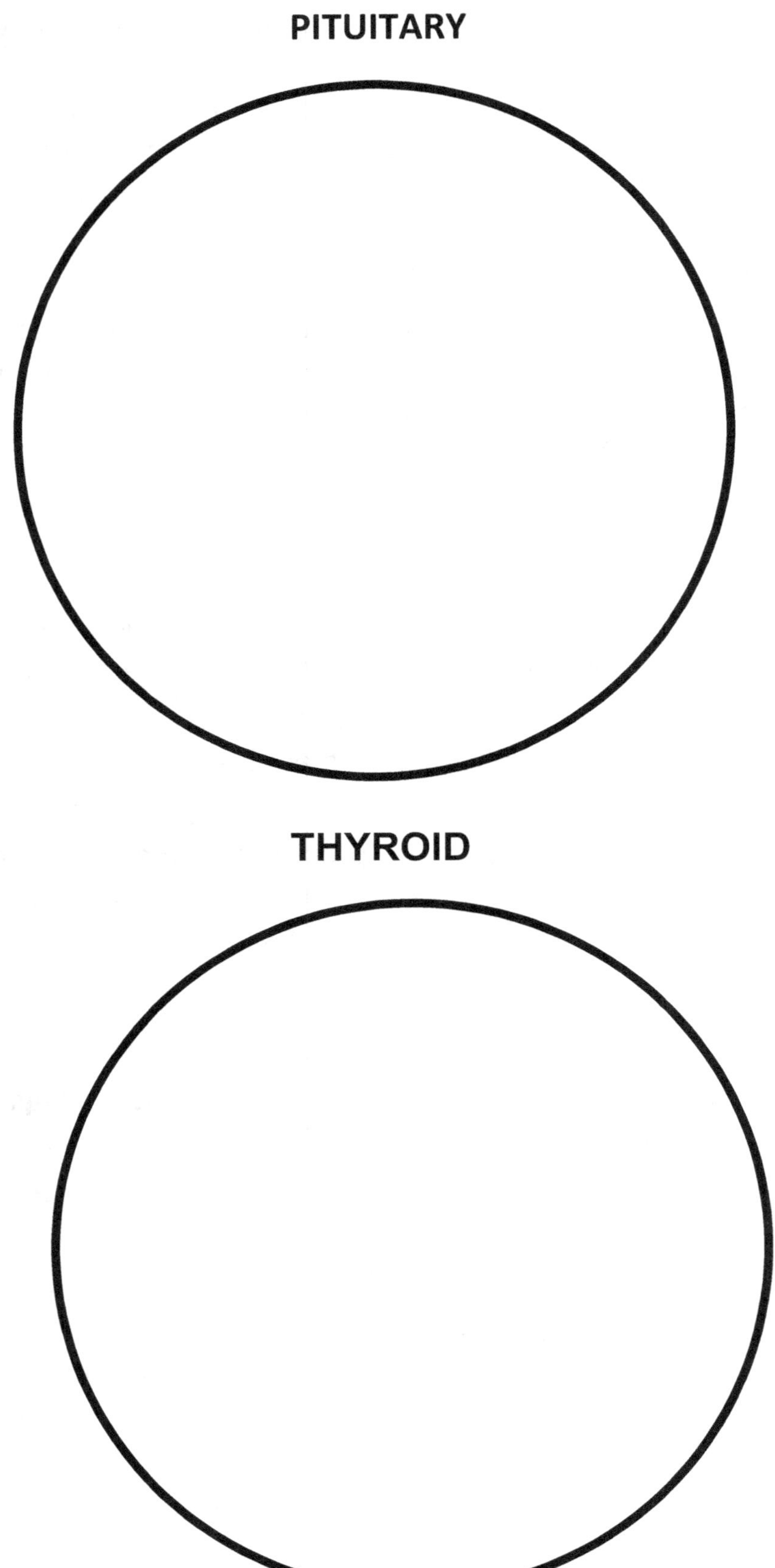

## THYROID

## PARATHYROID

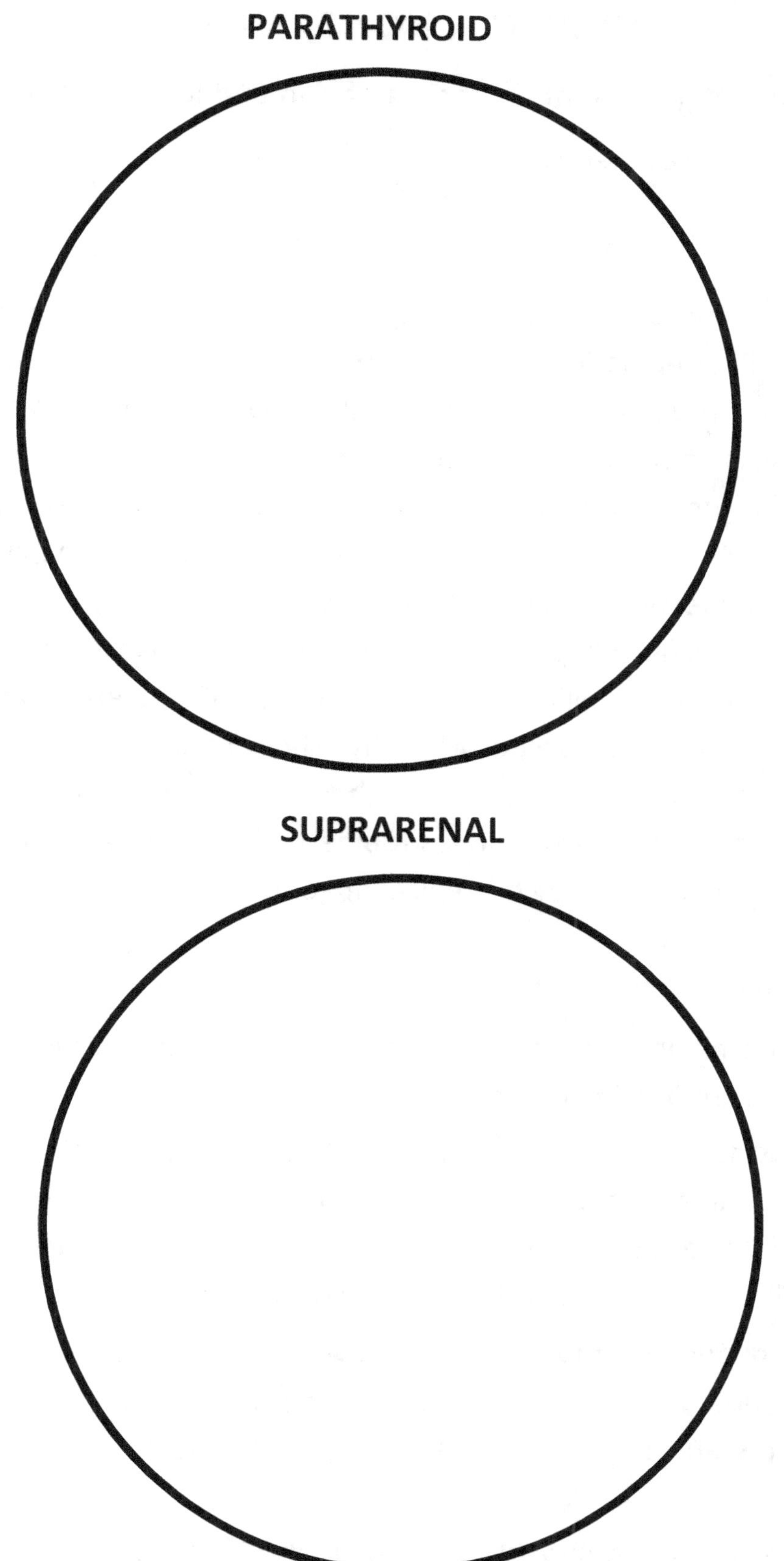

## SUPRARENAL

# CHAPTER NO.17 – INTEGUMENTARY SYSTEM

Integumentary system comprises of skin and its derivatives such as Nails, Hair, Sweat gland and Sebaceous glands.

## 1. SKIN

Skin is the protective covering of the entire body and has many important functions like regulation of heat, production of sweat, a sensory organ etc. It is water proof and in fact skin does not allow bacterial invasion.

Skin consists of two parts DERMIS and EPIDERMIS.

At the junction of the dermis and epidermis the dermis sends in finger like projection into the epidermis. These are called dermal papillae. Dermal papillae contain connective tissue, blood vessels nerves, lymphatics etc. to supply epidermis. The dermal papillae also fix the epidermis to the dermis by interlocking action of dermal papillae and invaginations of epidermis into the dermis. This epidermis cannot be peeled off easily. The epidermis also shows very fine ridges specially on palms and soles where they form typical patterns for each individual. The study of these dermal ridges (epidermal) has lot of importance in crime Dept to identify the criminal by his typical finger print pattern.

### EPIDERMIS

Epidermis is composed of stratified squamous epithelium. These layers are arranged from outside to inside as follows.

1) **Stratum Corneum** - Thick layer of cornified cells. The cellular details are not seen. The cells are dead with no nuclei. This layer appears pink. The cells are flattened scale like which are held together by lipid, hence non permeable to water. The cells contain hard protein, keratin.

2) **Stratum Lucidum** - 2 to 3 layer thick consisting of cells with indistinct borders and flattened nuclei. This layer is present in part of the skin which is thick as is palms and soles, the cells are highly retractile. The layer appears as clear space.

3) **Stratum Granulosum** - Consists of 2 to 4 layers of cells which are clearly

seen and contain granules in their cytoplasm. The cells are spindle shaped and granules are stained with haematoxyllin heavily, these are keratohyaline granules.

    4) **Stratum Germinivatum** - (Malphighi) - Consists of two parts.

    a) **Prickle cell layer** - Consisting of 5 to 8 layers of prickle cells. Polyhedral cells with spiny processes; The cells of this layer are attached to one another by desmosomes which retract during processing and give appearance like spines. Hence the name prickle cell layer.

    b) **Basal cell layer** - This is single row of columnar cells which rest on the basement membrane. These cells proliferate and newly formed cells migrate towards the surface to replace the cells constantly shed from stratum corneum. Hence it is also called germinal layer.

    Amongst these cells are the pigment cells (Melanoblasts) which contain varying amount of pigment, which is responsible for giving colour to the skin. Melanocytes are cells; with branching processes which make contact with prickle cells and transfer melanin to them.

## DERMIS

    Dermis is mainly composed of a very thick network of collagen and elastic, fibers embedded in the network are the hair follicles, sweat glands, sebaceous glands, nerve endings, adipose tissue, muscle fibres, blood vessels and lymphatics.

    Dermis projects into the epidermis as small papillae (Dermal Papillae). This is called papillary layer. Deep to this, is reticular layer which consists of thick collagen bundles and few adipocytes.

## Appendages of Skin

Appendages of skin are hairs, nails, sweat glands, sebaceous gland, etc.

    **Hairs** - Hairs are present all over body except palms and soles and some parts of external genitalia. Hairs are less in human being in comparison to other animals. The hairs in other animals help to keep the body temperature. This function has been taken over by adipose tissue in human being. Hence hairs are less. Short and sparse hairs with rich nerve supply of their roots makes the skin remarkable sensory organ.

Each hair has a visible part outside the body which is called shaft. The other part is embedded in the thickness of the skin and it is called root. The root has expanded lower end called bulb. The bulb is invaginated by dermis called hair papilla.

Hair roots are always attached to the skin obliquely; the hair can be structurally compared to stratum corneum consisting of dead cells. The cells of hair contain pigment melanin which gives colour to hair, also minute air bubbles are present among cells which influence the colour of hair, with age the pigment become less and the bubbles increase in number.

Hair is fixed in epidermis by its invagination into the dermis forming the hair follicle which surrounds the root of the hair. Hair follicle is nothing but epidermis invaginated along with the root of the hair in the dermis forming a sort of capsule to the root.

### Arrector Pilorum Muscles:

It is smooth muscle. One end attached to dermal papilla the other to the root of hair at the obtuse angle of root hair. Sebaceous gland lies in the angle between the Arrector pilorum muscle and hair follicle. Muscle is supplied by sympathetic nerve. Contraction causes straightening of hair shafts, depression of skin surrounding the hair and helping the secretions of sebaceous gland squeeze into the hair follicle.

**Sebaceous Gland** - Are always situated near the hair follicle and secrete an oily material known as sebum. The cells are large cells. The gland is Holocrine, there are number of alveoli lined by large polyhedral cells. No lumen is seen as the alveoli are filled with cells. A large duct open into the hair follicle:

**Sweat Gland** - These are the simple tubular glands which are coiled at their lower ends. These secrete sweat, which is poured out through minute pores on the surface of skin, by a duct. The secretary part of the gland, which lies in Dermis consists of the alveoli lined by cuboidal or polygonal cells. The duct runs from gland through dermis to epidermis and open on surface.

### Identification of the slide of Skin:
1) Note the two portions of skin i.e. epidermis and dermis.

2) **Epidermis** - See the stratified squamous epithelium, stratum corneum is seen as bundles of fibrin on cellular structure. Lucidum may be seen, as a homogeneous layer of cells without nuclei or it present occasionally flattened. The stratum granulosum cells are seen clearly, with granules in their  cytoplasm, darkly stained with haematoxylin. Deeper to stratum granulosum will be seen 3 to 4 layers of cells of stratum Malpighi. Pigment cells are seen at the stratum basale.

3) **Dermis** - You will find a large network of connective tissue fibres. See the hair follicles, sweat gland and sebaceous glands.
Arrectorpilorum muscle is seen. Dermal papillae are clearly seen.

4) **Skin Scalp** - Structure will be the same as above. Numerous hair follicles are seen with large amount of sebaceous glands.

## SKIN (Thick)

## Skin (Thin)

## CHAPTER NO. 18 -  ORGANS OF SPECIAL SENSES

## 1. <u>CORNEA</u>

This consists of five layers. they are from outside to inside

b) **Stratified squamous epithelium** non keratinised 3 to 4 layers of cells. Basal cells columnar middle layer polygonal and surface cells flattened; very regularly arranged parallel to the surface. Corneal epithelium regenerates rapidly after damage.

c)  **Anterior homogenous layer** (anterior limiting lamina or Bowman's lamina).

d) **Corneal stroma** consists of fibrous lamina 50 to 60 in number embedded in them are the fibroblasts. Collagen fibers are embedded in a ground substance which is mucoprotein. Collagen fibres are very regularly arranged and refractive index of collagen fibers and ground substance is same hence the transparency of cornea. Cornea has no blood vessels. It is avascular. It receives nutrition by diffusion from peripheral blood vessels. Cornea has rich nerve supply.

e) **Posterior limiting lamina** as a homogeneous layer (Descemet's membrane).

f)  **Single layer of cuboidal cells or flattened cells** which form the endothelium of anterior chamber. Cornea is transparent and avascular.


**Slide of Cornea** - Note all the layers. Fibroblasts in the substantiapropria can be identified by their nuclei.

## 2. <u>RETINA</u>

It is the innermost lining of the eyeball for perception of light stimuli. It is a nervous coat. Nerve fibres come out from the inner side of the retina. i.e. Rods and cones are on the outer side.

There are ten layers. They are from without inwards as follows.

1) **Pigment layer**. Cuboidal cells containing dark pigment. Each cell covers about 10 to 12 rods and cones.

2) **Layer of rods and cones**, these are the dendrites of photoreceptor cells. These

dendrite, contain photoreceptor substances.

3) **Outer limiting membrane**. Expanded outer fibres of neuroglial cells.

4) **Outer Nuclear Layer** - This is a layer of Nuclei of the rods and cones cells.

5) **Outer Plexiform Layer** - This is a layer consisting of network of synapses between the axons of rods and cones and dendrites of bipolar cells.

**Layer No. 2, 4, 5 constitute the First Neurone:**

The cells are photoreceptor rods and cone cells which are responsible for vision and colour vision.

6) **Inner Nuclear Layer** - These are the cell bodies of bipolar cells and neuroglial cells.

7) **Inner Plexiform Layer** - This is a synaptic layer of Axons of Bipolar cells and the dendrites of ganglion cells.

8) **Layer of Ganglion Cells** -large multipolar neurones.

9) **Optic Nerve Fibers** - These are the axons of the ganglion cells. All these fibres are collected together to form optic nerve.

10) **Internal Limiting Membrane** - Is formed by the expansion of the termination of inner fibres of neuroglial cells.

**Three neurones of Retina**.

a) Photoreceptor cells of rods and cones.

b) Bipolar cells of inner nuclear layer.

c) Ganglion cells.

## CORNEA

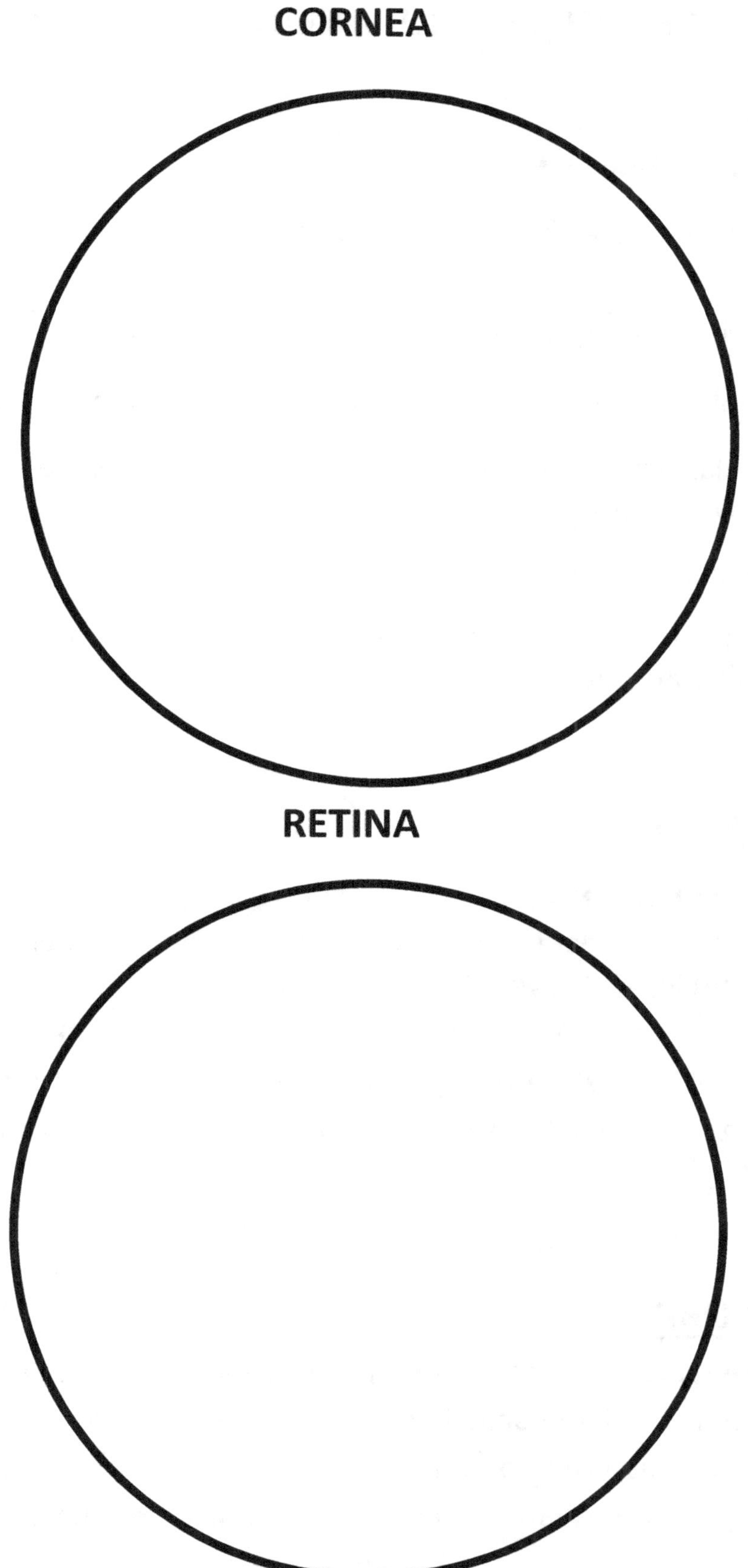

## RETINA

# CHAPTER NO.19 - NERVOUS SYSTEM

## 1. CEREBRUM

**Six layers of cerebral cortex**

1. Molecular layer- Outermost layer by piamater. It shows few nuclei of horizontal cells.

2. Outer granular layer- It contains many granule (stellate) cells.

3. Outer pyramidal layer- It contains many pyramidal cells and few granule cells.

4. Inner granular layer- It contains many granule (stellate) cells. It is densely populated by neurons.

5. Inner pyramidal layer- Large sized pyramidal cells are seen in this layer.

6. Polymorph layer- It is the last layer at grey white junction and shows nuclei of fusiform and Martinotti neurons.

## 2. CEREBELLUM

### Try to see three layers -
1) Outermost molecular layer, cells few; fibres more very faintly stained.
2) Middle Purkinje cell layer. (Single layer of cells).
3) Granular layer small cells with darkly stained nuclei are packed in this layer.

This punkinje cells are large flask shaped with dendrites coming out at the mouth of the flask like a branching tree. Axon comes out at base. Purkinje cells are identifying feature of cerebellum.

## 3. SPINAL CORD

White matter is present on the surface and grey matter in the central part. The white matter of the spinal cord is divided by posterior median septum and anterior median fissure into right and left halves. The white matter of each side is divided into posterior, lateral and anterior funiculi by the posterior and anterior horn and posterior median septum. The lateral funiculus is present between anterior and posterior horns. The anterior funiculus is present between anterior horn & anterior median fissure.

A narrow canal extends throughout the spinal cord into the centre of the cord and contains cerebro-spinal fluid. It is called central canal.

**Gray Matter** - Disposed off around the central canal in the form of 'H' Vertical limbs of 'H' represent the anterior and posterior horns. Horizontal limb is the grey commissure. The posterior horn is narrow and extends up to the surface of the cord. The anterior horn is wider and does not reach the surface. Hence' Posterior Funiculus is completely separate between two posterior horns. While anterior and lateral funiculi form continuous antero-lateral funiculus .

Lateral horn of the grey matter, is situated opposite the lateral ends of the grey commissure and is the main feature of the spinal cord from first thoracic to first lumbar segments of spinal cord only.

The cells of the lateral horn contain sympathetic neurons. Their axons go along with anterior nerve roots.

Cells of posterior horns are of smaller size. They are sensory cells. On the top of the posterior horn there is a cap like collection of faintly stained cells, which is known as substantia gelatinosa.

**White Matter** - Consists of medullated nerve fibres arranged in bundles (tracts) which are ascending and descending. There are no nerve cells in the white matter of spinal cord.

## CEREBRUM

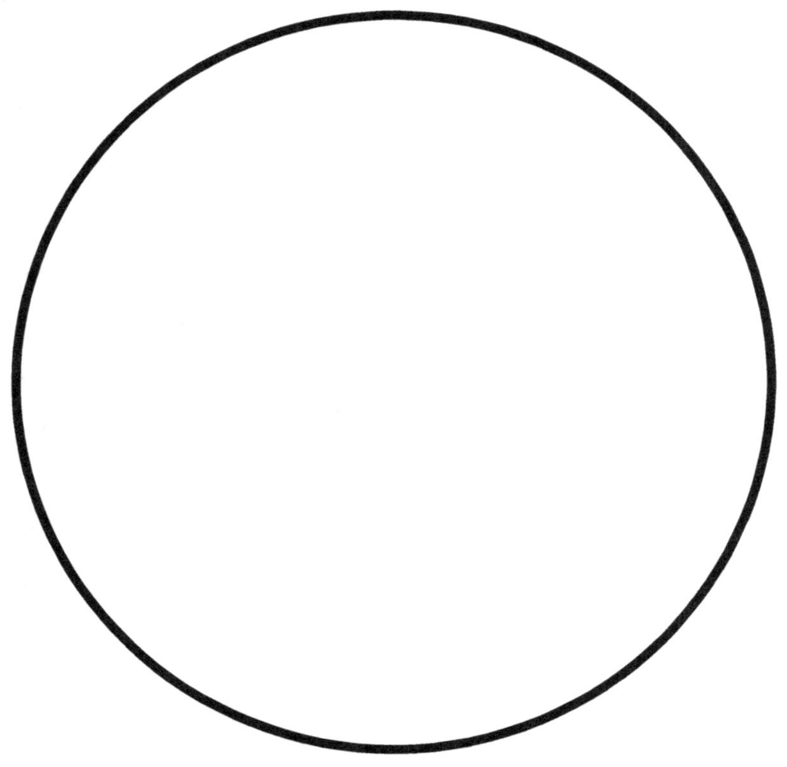

## CEREBELLUM

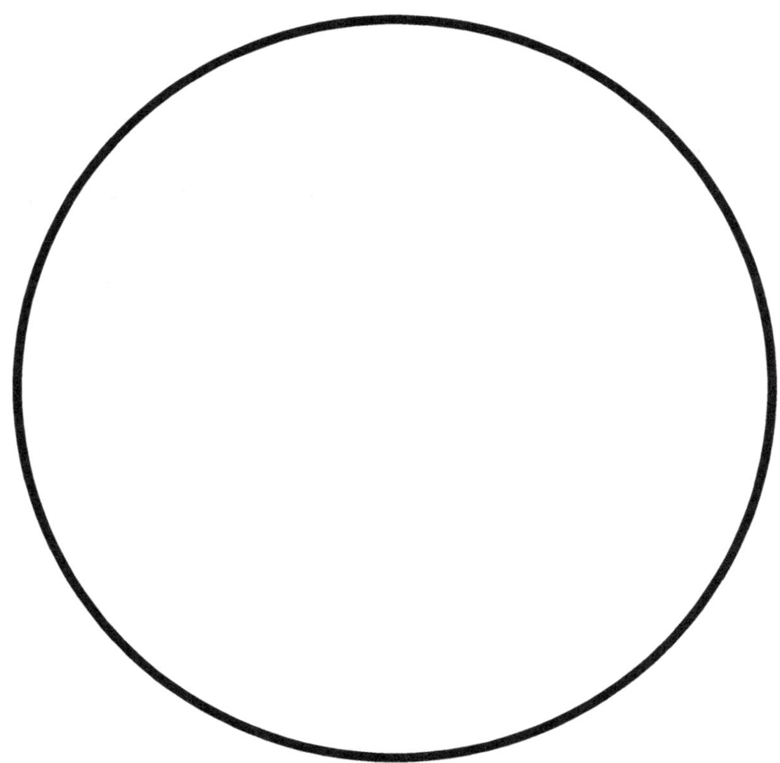

## SPINAL CORD

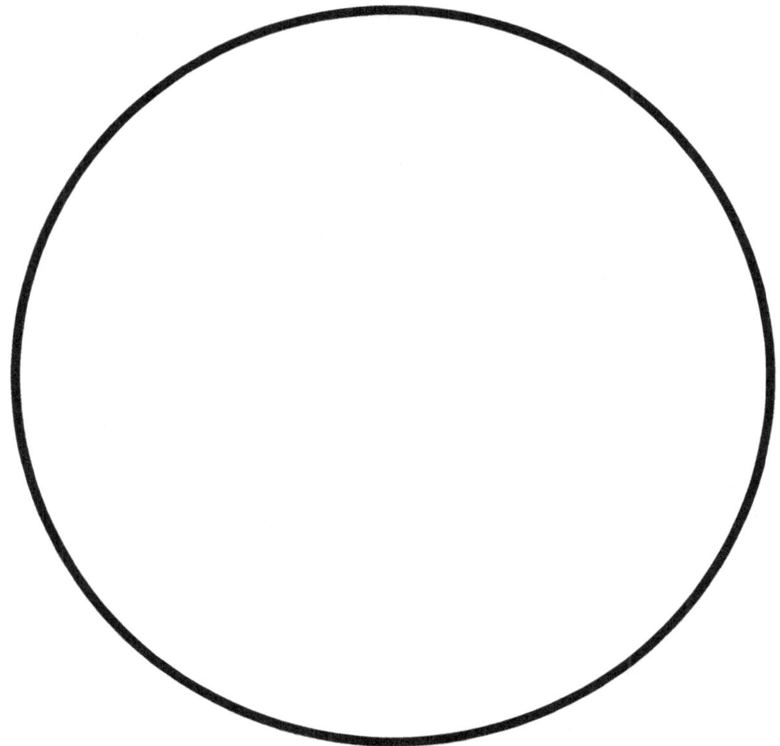

www.ingramcontent.com/pod-product-compliance
Lightning Source LLC
Chambersburg PA
CBHW081615250726

48657CB00009B/2580